Old Testament and
Christian Preaching

Old Testament and Christian Preaching

Hans Walter Wolff

Fortress Press   Philadelphia

Translated by Margaret Kohl

Library of Congress Cataloging-in-Publication Data
Wolff, Hans Walter.
  Old Testament and Christian preaching.

  1. Bible. O.T.—Sermons. 2. Sermons, English—
Translations from German. 3. Sermons, German—
Translations into English. 4. Bible. O.T.—
Hermeneutics. I. Title.
BS1151.5.W64 1986   252   85-45477
ISBN 0-8006-1905-6

K903K85   Printed in the United States of America   1-1905

Contents

Preface   7

Acknowledgments   9

1. "I Will Make Him a Helper . . ."   11

2. Sodom and Gomorrah   19

3. Stop!   27

4. The Essential Prayer   39

5. Someone in Despair   45

6. The Dawn of Peace   55

7. The Hope of the Disappointed   65

8. The Church—A Hopeless Case   73

9. For Theologians Only!   83

10. This Ship Is Sinking!   91

11. Disputed Old Testament   103

12. Some Thoughts on the Typological Interpretation of the Old Testament   107

Preface

This volume presents a collection of sermon-meditations from one of the outstanding Old Testament scholars of our time. Professor Hans Walter Wolff, an emeritus of the distinguished Theological Faculty of Heidelberg University, provides us with a selection of his sermons which span two decades of his work as biblical commentator, professor, and preacher. Professor Wolff is already well-known to students of the Old Testament in this country through his scholarly articles, monographs, and especially his commentaries on the Minor Prophets. In this English translation of sermons preached in university chapel, church, and theological seminary, the author demonstrates his passionate conviction that careful exegetical study of the biblical text stands in the service of, and leads toward, Christian proclamation.

Hans Walter Wolff began his teaching career at the Kirchliche Hochschule in Wuppertal in 1947 while still a pastor. He became professor of Old Testament at Wuppertal in 1951, then taught at Mainz from 1959 until 1967, when he was called to Heidelberg to succeed his mentor and friend, Gerhard von Rad. During his career in the university, his work did not focus merely on the academic: his highly acclaimed, technical commentaries were inevitably accompanied by volumes of sermons as well as Bible studies for lay audiences. Thus, for example, his Hermeneia commentary *Hosea* was followed by two books of sermons on texts from Hosea; his commentary on Amos (*Joel and Amos*, Hermeneia) was accompanied by a collection of expository articles and sermons (*Die Stunde des Amos. Prophetie und Protest*, 5th ed. [Munich: Chr. Kaiser Verlag, 1981]); parallel to his commentary on Micah, *Dodekapropheton Mica* (Neukirchen-Vluyn: Neukirchener Verlag, 1982), appeared a volume of studies written chiefly for an audience of non-specialists (*Micah the Prophet* [Philadelphia: Fortress Press, 1982]). Hardly a picture of the "ivory-tower theologian," Wolff understands his work ultimately to serve the interests of Christian proclamation in and for the church.

The sermons offered in the present volume, says the author, "are meant to render an account." That is, they illustrate how one moves from scholarly exegesis, with its philological and historical focus, to Christian preaching. It is his conviction that all tools available to the biblical exegete must be used to discern what the text intended to say to its original audience. He writes, "It is impossible to expend too much industry on trying to discover with all the means available what the biblical words actually say and want to convey" (p. 103). Only by painstaking study can the preacher avoid the danger of reading preconceived notions and alien ideas into the text.

But is Christian preaching from the Old Testament, even with careful textual study, so uncomplicated for us today? What kind of hermeneutic can best guide us in understanding and preaching Old Testament pericopes? Professor Wolff rejects the idea that the Old Testament has little or nothing to say to twentieth-century Christians, as well as the notion that its message speaks to us directly, without reference to Jesus Christ. While Wolff follows no "generally valid recipe" for preaching from the Old Testament, he does keep to three simple rules: inquire carefully into the historical meaning of the text to grasp its intention; compare the text with corresponding New Testament passages; apply the text's kerygma to the contemporary hearers in ways appropriate to the original intention of the passage. In spite of misunderstandings which have arisen concerning the word "typological," Wolff retains this term as appropriately descriptive of his hermeneutic. The reader will find a succinct and helpful discussion of typological exposition in the final two chapters of the volume.

The sermons presented here are commended to laypersons, seminary students, teachers of homiletics, as well as biblical scholars. All readers will find here an uncommon liveliness of language and richness of theological insight which, when combined, make for provocative, forceful, and contemporary preaching of the gospel.

GARY STANSELL
St. Olaf College

Acknowledgments

Chapters 2–8, 11, and 12 appeared originally in *wie eine Fackel* copyright © 1980 Neukirchener Verlag, Neukirchen-Vluyn, Federal Republic of Germany.

Chapter 1 appeared originally as "Der mensch und seine Hilfe" in *Menschliches* © 1971 Chr. Kaiser Verlag, Munich, Federal Republic of Germany.

Chapter 9 appeared originally as "Nur fur Theologen" in *Die Hochzeit der Hure* © 1979 Chr. Kaiser Verlag, Munich, Federal Republic of Germany.

Chapter 10 appeared originally as "Die Schiff sinkt" in *Die Stunde des Amos* © 1966 Chr. Kaiser Verlag, Munich, Federal Republic of Germany.

Selections from Dietrich Bonhoeffer, *Letters and Papers from Prison*, Copyright © 1953, 1967, 1971 by SCM Press, Ltd., London, are reprinted by permission of SCM Press, Ltd. and Macmillan Publishing Company.

1

"I Will Make Him a Helper . . ."

Sermon on Genesis 2:15, 18–23*

The Lord God took the man and put him in the garden of Eden to till it and
keep it. . . .
Then the Lord God said, "It is not good that the man should be alone; I will
make him a helper who corresponds to him." So out of the ground the Lord
God formed every beast of the field and every bird of the air, and brought them
to the man to see what he would call them; and whatever the man called every
living creature, that was its name. The man gave names to all cattle, and to the
birds of the air, and to every beast of the field; but for the man there was not
found a helper that corresponded to him. So the Lord God caused a deep
sleep to fall upon the man, and while he slept took one of his ribs and closed up
its place with flesh; and the rib which the Lord God had taken from the man he
made into a woman and brought her to the man. Then the man said,

> "This at last
> is bone of my bones
>   and flesh of my flesh;
> she shall be called Woman,
>   because she was taken out of Man."

What we have just heard is one of the most splendid and at the same
time one of the most intimate stories in the Bible. Isn't it particularly
fitting for two biologists, this story about the man who has to plant his
garden and look after it, the man to whom all the animals are brought
so that he can give them their names, and who finally discovers his true
partner? What we find here is a very archaic view of the relationship
between human beings and animals, and between man and woman. It
makes us want to listen to the story, to find out what impact a three-

---

*Preached at the wedding of two biologists.

thousand-year-old biblical word has on us. It makes us want to discover and think about the truth it holds for us, and for you.

"Then the Lord God said, 'It is not good that the human being should be alone.'" These words belong to the framework of the story about the man who has been created so that he may cultivate and care for the garden (vv. 8–9, 15). But the Bible really, and very wisely, talks about *the human being*. For later listeners the saying applies to the woman as well as to the man. The words are very old, but they reflect nothing of the patriarchal pride of the first man to be created. No, he is unhappy and unsatisfied. For he is alone. The lonely woman will feel just the same. She can listen together with the man to what is true for both of them; as the Lord God said, "It is not good for the human being to be alone."

His God sympathizes with him. The God who is speaking is not the omniscient and perfect God of the philosophers. This is the God of the open questions, the God who sees people's distresses, the God who—as we see most clearly of all in Jesus—suffers with men and women under all the things that are not good. But not only that. In the midst of all the imperfections, God sets to work directly on human beings' behalf.

"I *will make him a helper who corresponds to him.*" Notice that the Bible doesn't talk about "a helpmeet who will care for him," as Luther's version once had it. Luther shared the view of marriage taken by the sociology of his time: he was thinking of the woman who is subordinate to her husband and who looks after his needs. But what is sought for here is mutual support. It is certainly not merely help in the garden that the Bible is thinking of. (Though what a pleasure that will be too! What a wonderful botanical garden you will be able to create between you!) Nor is the idea behind the passage that this is the only way in which children can be born—though of course it is true that the solitary person remains an unfruitful person. "A helper that corresponds to him": the Old Testament often lays great stress on the blessing of children, but this saying is a long way away from that. God's solicitous care is directed first of all to seeing that two people who fit together can be wholly there for one another. The Old Testament has a number of things to say in other passages as well about the inner meaning of a life shared by two people. When Hannah, who was to become the mother of Samuel, is weeping over her childlessness, her husband Elkanah says to her:

"Hannah, why is your heart sad? Am I not more to you than ten sons?" That one of you can mean more to the other than ten children—you young people will be able to discover that together. And those of us who are growing old, and becoming lonelier again, would do well to remember it from time to time too. In Deut. 24:5 the Old Testament law decrees that a newly married man does not have to go to war with the army. He is to be free for a whole year "to devote himself to his wife whom he has taken." We are reminded of an old saying about marriage: "To have time for your companion is more important than to have money for him." After all, a horse, an angora cat, or a parakeet can all be had for money too.

The gift of a shared life is thought of in the first place as mutual help, help in the form of a proper counterpart, a correspondence. Old Testament Wisdom knows how needy we are. I cannot resist reading you some verses from the Book of Ecclesiastes (4:9–12):

> Two are better than one.
> For if they fall,
>   the one can lift up the other.
> But woe to him who is alone when he falls,
>   and has not another to lift him up.
> Again, if two lie together,
>   they are warm;
> but how can one
>   be warm alone?
> And if a man attacks the one,
>   then both offer him resistance.

Help when we fall, help when we are shivering, help against hostility: this is what one person is supposed to be for the other, first of all. One person gives the other security and a sense of safekeeping in their mutual understanding. One is a rock for the other. However much the relation of man and wife has changed throughout the centuries—and however much it changes in the future—this is the Creator's intention, which you have to discover: "a help that fits the other."

But in spite of this it is by no means a matter of course when a person finds the helper who really does correspond to him. Drawing on an accumulated store of wisdom and experience, and out of trust in God's

13

goodness and liberty, our age-old story goes on to tell how the Creator went to work:

> So out of the ground the Lord God formed every beast of the field and every bird of the air, and brought them to the man to see what he would call them; and whatever the man called every living creature, that was its name. The man gave names to all cattle, and to the birds of the air, and to every beast of the field.

We are hearing about the beginning of zoology. The creation of living things is not human beings' affair; but their discovery and classification undoubtedly are. It was during your biology studies, during a practical course in animal identification, that you found one another. Do I remember rightly that it was insects first of all, from bugs to cockchafers, that you were concerned with? You were out looking for chironomids in their various habitats, from the Rhine plain to the hills of the Black Forest. You biologists know all the things the world of creation holds for human beings—food, medicines, things to lighten our workload. God has given human beings a world full of riches. They have not nearly discovered or fully interpreted all the resources that world has to offer. They have their hands full with warding off the terrible damage which human beings themselves have destructively and devastatingly imposed on the world of creation. This will be enough to fill your professional lives—to enter into the endless wealth of the created world of plants and animals, exploring it and protecting it.

But the Bible has something more to say still about the realms of botany and zoology: "But for the human being he did not find the help that would have corresponded to him." There is no partner to be found here—no partner for conversation, or silent understanding, no partner to love. So in spite of all the things that have been discovered, the tension has simply built up even more since that first discovery of all: that it is not good to be alone. It is an experimenting God who is at work, not the eternal, foreknowing providence of the school theologians. He makes his experiments for human beings and with them. As Jesus of Nazareth did, he accompanies them in their daily workaday lives. If we consider what God's purpose really was, then what he had made up to now must be provisionally judged a failure. But what a tremendous enrichment it was for men and women all the same! Even in his apparent failures, we discover God as the One who gives abundantly until the cup runs over. The ancient story has this to tell us as well, though by the way.

Does every human life repeat something of that long, tense, expectant path, with its enriching and yet unsatisfying encounters? Does the series of created things which is presented to Adam extend still further, with "provisional" human beings too? Are there not splendid specimens which prove after all to be only attractive "birds of the air," deluxe editions of "the beasts of the field," not the really appropriate and corresponding helper? What is to be done if the wealth of types does not after all satisfy the longing for the true counterpart?

> So the Lord God caused a deep sleep to fall upon the man, and while he slept took one of his ribs and closed up its place with flesh; and the rib which the Lord God had taken from the man he made into a woman and brought her to the man.

Here our God reveals himself as the One who truly gives away the bride, as the One who helps the human being to the final discovery he has hitherto longed for in vain. Who else could have done it? Who else can still do it for any one of us? But how does it begin? With a deep sleep! What does this sleep mean? The ironical old verse is wide of the mark:

> While Adam slept, Eve from his side arose.
> Strange his first sleep should be his last repose.

No, another line is far more apt:

> Heaven's last best *gift*, my ever new delight! . . .

exclaims Adam to the woman in Milton's *Paradise Lost* (Book 5). The story about the deep sleep into which God cast the man so effectively draws on very ancient notions about anatomy and surgery and anesthesia. But these very ideas make it drastically clear that the man's true partner materializes entirely without any human activity. The man is completely passive. He cannot even watch as this unique being is made. When she is brought to him there she stands, finished and complete. And this is exactly in accordance with your own experience.

The ancient storyteller opens our eyes for something else as well. The other—the counterpart—is not made out of earthly elements like all the animals. She is created from the rib of the man himself. Although he is

completely inactive as the other comes into being, the two belong together from the very beginning. Each one of them lacks something essential as long as he fails to find the person who belongs to him from his
very origin. How does the incomplete person become whole and complete once more? "God brought the woman to the man." What the human being didn't plan, what he hasn't calculated on, what he didn't
even see as it came into being has become a confronting event.

Then the bridegroom's jubilation breaks forth:

> This at last
> is bone of my bones
> and flesh of my flesh.

The very rhythms leap for joy. People who are unknown to one another
discover each other as the closest of relations. In your case there are
even some special little signs of belongingness. Doesn't being born on
the same day mean being born for one another? So it was with you. So
the joy breaks out: at last we are a whole person, a person who is
helped in the appropriate way, a person who knows that he is understood. Now we have a twofold freedom, freedom for two. To be in relation to one another means fulfillment. Martin Buber says: "I become
through my relation to the Thou."

The world around sees this happiness of belonging:

> She shall be called Woman,
> because she was taken out of Man.

(It is hardly possible to express more exactly the close verbal relationship between the Hebrew *ish* and *ishah*, which is a linguistic reproduc-
tion of the essential relationship between man and woman.) We should
notice that here the man does not give his wife her name, as he did with
the animals. Here again we find an antipatriarchal feature in the story.
There is no trace here of dependence or domination, let alone suppres-
sion. This is an expression of pure joy at belonging together. This is the
beginning—and your beginning too.

But doesn't the Bible know the other side too?

> Your desire shall be for your husband,
> but he shall rule over you!
>
> (Gen. 3:16)

16

And in fact this comes out in the very next chapter, when mistrust has led these two human beings astray. The woman's sufferings under her husband are apparently a result of the Fall. But the Bible will tell us about the man's suffering too, in the Book of Proverbs, for example:

> It is better to live in a corner of the housetop
> than in a house shared with a contentious woman.
>
> (Prov. 21:9)

You too should soberly face the fact that the person you have married is not the perfect ideal of a human being. Is it not likely that with you too there will be disappointments, altercations, and other plagues? That one or the other of you will perhaps be domineering or opinionated? The Bible teaches us to be realistic.

But then what does it mean when we read: "What God has joined together let no man put asunder" (Matt. 19:6)? What is the real meaning of your intention, and your public, mutual promise not to leave one another until death divides you? Isn't this the threat of an institutional straitjacket, if estrangement begins to build up dividing walls between you? But every delight covets eternity. Love longs for permanent, reliable security and safekeeping. How can we human beings escape the conflict between the compulsions that imprison us and what we really desire?

Here the message of the New Testament encounters us as a liberating solution. Torn as we are between our compulsions and our true desires, the total forgiveness of Christ and the new creation of the One who truly loves make it possible for us to expect to leave behind us day by day our unsatisfied, divided selves. Every one of us will self-critically admit with Paul: "not that I have already obtained this." But each of us, too, can go on: "but I press on to make it my own, because Christ Jesus has made me his own" (Phil. 3:12). Two people who in Christ's name set out with one another on their way, preserve one another from inner stagnation or even regression. Christ accepts us with the supreme power of his love; for the tangible help of his word is at hand and we can daily ask for the overmastering power of his Spirit. So we can do no more than follow the counsel we have been given: "Accept one another as Christ has accepted us" (Rom. 15:7). The person who is unable to find the first word after a quarrel should not marry, says a wise old saying.

Dostoevsky once wrote: "To love someone means seeing him as God meant him to be." Jesus' word and Spirit disclose to you two a new vision of one another. You will again and again be able to rediscover each other as God meant you to be for one another. Both of you can learn every day to see the other as a gift, and also as a task for one another. And then the ancient bridegroom's jubilation will sound for you in untold new variations:

> This at last
> is bone of my bones
> and flesh of my flesh.

Each discovers the other as the one who needs his help; and each discovers himself as the one who needs the help of the other. And in both we discover God as the One who brings us together.

In this way, in forgiving love, we shall be safe, whole, and healthful human beings. It is a strange and astonishing mystery that in marriage we can grow even from our faults and failings if we do not reject the creative power of the word of Jesus that lays hold of us. The wisdom of love says:

> Marriage needs faith.
> What if there were two
> and he were not in the midst of them?

This is the beginning of the new world on this ancient planet. May it be the beginning of your home too.

2

Sodom and Gomorrah

Sermon on Genesis 19:1—29*

The two messengers came to Sodom in the evening; and Lot was sitting in the gate of Sodom. When Lot saw them, he rose to meet them, and bowed himself with his face to the earth, and said, "My lords, turn aside, I pray you, to your servant's house and spend the night, and wash your feet; then you may rise up early and go on your way." They said, "No; we will spend the night in the street." But he urged them strongly; so they turned aside to him and entered his house; and he made them a feast, and baked unleavened bread, and they ate.

But before they lay down, the men of the city, the men of Sodom, both young and old, all the people to the last man, surrounded the house; and they called to Lot, "Where are the men who came to you tonight? Bring them out to us, that we may have intercourse with them." Lot went out of the door to the men, shut the door after him, and said, "I beg you, my brothers, do not act so wickedly. Behold, I have two daughters who have never had intercourse with any man; let me bring them out to you, and do to *them* as you please; only do nothing to these men, for they have come under the shelter of my roof for that reason." But they said: *gesh hāle 'āh!* ("Get lost!"). And they said, "This fellow came here as a stranger, and he would play the judge! Now we will deal worse with you than with them." Then they pressed hard against the man Lot, and drew near to break open the door. But the men put forth their hands and brought Lot into the house to them, and shut the door. And they struck with blindness the men who were at the door of the house, both small and great, so that they gave up trying to find the door. Then the two men said to Lot, "Have you anyone else here? A son-in-law? Your sons? Your daughters? Or have you anyone belonging to you in the city? Bring them out of the place; for we are about to destroy this place, because the outcry against its people has become great before the Lord, and the Lord has sent us to destroy it." So Lot went out and said to his sons-in-law, who were to marry his daughters, "Up, get *out* of this place; for the Lord is about to destroy the city." But he seemed to his sons-in-law to be jesting.

*Preached in the university service in the Peterskirche, Heidelberg, on Remembrance Day, November 16, 1975, the penultimate Sunday in the church year.

When morning dawned, the messengers urged Lot to hurry, saying, "Arise, take your wife and your two daughters who are here, lest you be consumed in the punishment of the city." But he lingered; so the men seized him and his wife and his two daughters by the hand, the Lord being merciful to him, and they brought him forth, and only set him free again outside the city.

And when they had brought them forth, he said: "Flee for your life; do not look back or stop anywhere in the whole valley; flee to the hills! Otherwise you will die." But Lot said to him, "Oh no, my Lord! Behold, your servant has found favor in your sight, and you have shown me great kindness in saving my life; but I cannot flee to the hills. I should faint. I should die. Behold yonder city nearby. I could flee there. It is a little one. I could escape there—is it not a little one?—and my life will be saved!" He said to him, "Yes, this favor also I will grant you, that I will not overthrow the city of which you have spoken. Make haste, escape there! for I can do nothing till you arrive there." Therefore the name of the city was called Zoar—"little one."

The sun had just risen over the earth and Lot had just arrived in Zoar. Then the Lord rained on Sodom and Gomorrah brimstone and fire from the Lord out of heaven; and he overthrew those cities, and all the valley, and all the inhabitants of the cities, and what grew on the ground. But Lot's wife, who was behind him, looked back, and she became a pillar of salt. And Abraham went early in the morning to the place where he had stood before the Lord; and he looked down toward Sodom and Gomorrah and toward all the land of the valley, and beheld, and lo, the smoke of the land went up like the smoke of a furnace. So it was that, when God destroyed the cities of the valley, God remembered Abraham, and sent Lot out of the midst of the overthrow, when he overthrew the cities in which Lot dwelt.

Surely a text for the film producers! Shooting could already be going on. For every one of us is already playing his role. The cast we can choose from is: Lot—a newcomer to Sodom; his wife; their two daughters; their two future sons-in-law; and two messengers who have arrived unexpectedly. Then, among the original inhabitants of Sodom itself, we have a number of homosexuals, some of them young, some of them senile. Last in the cast is the old man Abraham. Some of us have even taken on two roles. Others of us are in the process of changing the roles we had chosen. And this is still possible. So we had better have a look at the film script.

Let us look for the main point first. What is the scarlet thread that runs through the scenes following the introduction? On the very evening of their arrival, the messengers tell Lot: "Get your people out of the city!" The same night Lot visits his sons-in-law and tells them: "You'd better leave!" The next morning the messengers urge Lot himself to get on his way. They take hold of him and drag him and the three women out. They only let them go when they are outside the city. Then they spur him on again: "Into the mountains! Keep going! It's a matter of life or death. Get away from here!" That is enough for the moment. This is evidently the theme of these opening scenes. It is essential to leave Sodom. Get out! Get out! That is the message that echoes and re-echoes through the text.

But why do these people have to leave so abruptly? The messengers explain why. Total annihilation is unavoidable and imminent. The accusations against Sodom cry out to high heaven. A few lurid pictures are enough. What the messengers themselves experience is worse than they expected. Evidently they wanted to sleep out of doors, so as to find out for themselves just how far things could go in this place. Now even the house where they have been so hospitably received is stormed. In order to protect the strangers, Lot is prepared to surrender his daughters to the debauchees. This painful episode shows the sinister way in which wrong breeds wrong. When Lot dares to stand up to his attackers, they knock him down. Breaking down the door with brute force, the men attempt to enter. It is all shameless, iniquitous. Then the messengers tell Lot: there is going to be an end of this rule of unbridled greed and violence. God is resolved. So leaving Sodom is a matter of life and death.

Today is Remembrance Day. What point does this day have? We are remembering far-off graves, and the fate of the missing who have never come back. For how many of us has the war made growing old more difficult, lonelier, more helpless? Thirty to thirty-five years ago, fire and brimstone rained down on our cities. Sodom was nothing but a little curtain-raiser in comparison. Do we older people grieve over the guilt we shared in making the tyranny of greed and violence possible? Do we grieve over our all-too-feeble resistance? Do you young people grieve with us older ones, that we have learnt so little since? Indeed, now some people have rebuilt their Sodom, and others their Gomorrah, although we were fortunate beyond all our deserts. Although? When all is said and done, Lot moved to Sodom because it offered better living conditions. Abraham had generously made the move possible: "If you take the left hand, then I will go to the right!" But it is in economic abundance, most of all, that hybris and lack of moderation flourish.

21

Today we are called to localize neither Lot's Sodom nor the Gomorrah of the Nazis. What we have to find out is where our own individual Sodom lies, and where we can discover our common Gomorrah. Let us look honestly at our dealings with other people, and with strangers now, today, while there is still time. Where, among ourselves, does unbridled greed and the lust for profit flourish? Or pleasure in violence, direct or indirect? Love makes us put ourselves in the place of other people. Where is this love pushed out by ruthlessness? Each of us should recognize his own Sodom.

But the church—yes, and a university congregation too—should not be blind to the public Sodom we all share. Even joy in physical sexuality is becoming demonic, because coitus is extorted without the will for coexistence. Sexuality is becoming an uncanny vortex which is dragging people down, threatening to divide body and soul and to destroy the love that comprehends them both. In exactly the same way, the misuse of sources of energy is poisoning the space we live in. The smog which we are recklessly and publicly fabricating is threatening to smother us in our own progress, perhaps quite soon. Party wrangles are fought out with a self-righteousness which degrades other people to enemies, even in the university, even in the church. The Christian church should unite in its sober diagnosis of things as they are: lustful greed and subtle forms of violence in all sectors of life are the dangers threatening our personal and public future.

Surely the story of our Sodom between 1933 and 1945 should count as sufficient warning? At that time people laughed at and despised the story of Sodom in the Book of Genesis; but they had to play out that story again in their own persons. Who today listens to God's word of warning which speaks to us from the Bible? Our history should surely tell us how difficult we men and women find it to change the roles we have chosen, although this very word of God should provide a helpful stimulus to us to do so.

This story mirrors four different reactions to the imposition of a clear and definite separation from our Sodom. First of all there are the sons-in-law. The notion that greed and violence inevitably draw down fire and brimstone on themselves seems to them ludicrous. They think that old Lot is an odd fish. This could well be the normal reaction of people today. There is no chance for a better future without force, people think.

Anyone who maintains anything different has to be joking. Don't let us make any mistake at this point: this means making a joke of nothing less than the cross of Christ. "Rather suffer injustice than commit it." People react to this, as they do to all threats of disaster: they think that they can ignore it and get on with the agenda. This is the reaction of the sons-in-law, then and now; the sons-in-law round about us and perhaps in us as well.

How does Lot himself react? Has he been affected by his thick-skinned sons-in-law? At all events, when morning comes the messengers have to urge him to hurry. "But he lingered," we are told. Lot has personality problems. He was able to assert his "territorial claims" toward his uncle, Abraham; and he acquired the better land to live in and for his economic purposes. Is he now supposed to leave all this behind? How little one can carry with one! Think of packing a suitcase if you have been expelled from the country, with only a few hours to leave, and if you can take only twenty pounds. What are all the things that make it so hard for us to leave our Sodom? Lot would probably never have made the move at all if the two messengers had not seized him and his wife and his two daughters, one of them in each hand, and dragged them out of the town. This is what things are like in Sodom. Then and now, round about us and in us. Even the best of us, relatively speaking, is someone who is divided in mind about what to do: "But Lot lingered." Without God's special commando unit he would soon have been standing in the midst of a rain of fire.

The sons-in-law laugh. Lot lingers. What is the third reaction? Outside the city the messengers let Lot go. He is away from the main danger zone. They give him new orders: "Don't stop! Don't look round! Make for the mountains!" But Lot feels faint at the very thought. "I can't! I can't manage those steep slopes." But he still has plenty of energy for long speeches. A typical intellectual perhaps, with a religious streak. Yes, he comments in some detail on the previous mercy of God. But he has a few special requests. Zoar is not far away. Admittedly, it is still on the fringe of the disaster area. But—Lot works it out for God—it is very small (hence the name Zoar). Couldn't this little village be saved from the fate of the big city? Lot is too feeble to manage any mountain peaks. He couldn't manage them then, and he can't manage them now, the Lot round about us and within us. And lo and behold, his request is granted! He is allowed to cut his march short. Only: "Make haste, escape there!"

Shortly after this there is another reaction still—the fourth. The whole scene is uncannily silent. Lot has just arrived in Zoar. Sodom is already in flames. But Lot's wife is still behind him. She looks back—and is petrified into a pillar of salt. This dimly lit scene is almost more horrible than the burning city. Why did this have to be? Was her heart still in Sodom, more than in the new life ahead? How well we can understand her longing then; how well we can understand the same longing in others and in ourselves. How often we have played a similar part. Still addicted to Sodom, even in its downfall.

What is the point of this terrible, wordless picture? Lot already stands in Zoar, in the daybreak of a rescued life. And his wife, just behind him, is petrified in the glow of Sodom's fires. This figure, in its unforgettable horror, intensifies everything that the previous scenes have tried to say: a complete severance is vitally necessary. The laughter of the sons-in-law dies away in the sulfurous rain. Lot lingers, but he lets himself be drawn forward. Lot achieves no mountain peak, but he makes his way toward Zoar. Lot's wife's glance back holds her spellbound. Picture after picture etch themselves indelibly into the reader's mind. It is essential that we leave Sodom behind both in an external and an internal sense. How often this has now been repeated! A repeated insistence on this message—that is what we need in the temptations of our assaulted, torn, slothful lives. The repetition of the word which once moved us is healing for our souls and keeps them on the right path.

But isn't what this biblical story asks of us really very unpopular? More, isn't it actually irresponsible nowadays? Does it not even make Pharisees of us? Well, the story is certainly written for endangered people in need of help, people for whom survival is anything but a matter of course. It certainly doesn't say everything that might be said about the problems of injustice and salvation. But what it does is surely this: 1) It defines every zone of injustice as a source of danger threatening life itself. 2) It demands an unambiguous dissociation from injustice. 3) It is passionately moved by concern for the people who are in danger.

As illustrations, let us remember three pictures. First of all, the picture

of Lot. Anyone who has reached his Zoar as Lot has certainly has nothing to boast about. His only contribution was indecision and laziness. If
he escaped the fiery embers, it was only because the two messengers
seized him by force, and because the way he had to take was mercifully
shortened. There is no room for Pharisaism here. But there is hope,
even for frail, half-hearted Christians. How do we show our gratitude for
this?

Then let us think of the second picture: the hands of the two messengers. First of all, when Lot was attacked they pulled him through the
barely open door into the safety of the house, and then they dragged
him out of the endangered city. What do we use our hands for? Should
we not keep them in good shape, to help people who are in danger,
too? It is we who have to refute the suspicion that we are washing our
hands of Sodom, not the narrator. Today we are being asked to give an
offering for young people who are undergoing prison sentences. Even if
our hands do not directly reach people who are endangered, we can at
least put them deeper into our pockets on their behalf.

The third picture: the old man Abraham, as he again looks out from
Mamre, gazing down on to the terrible landscape. At the end, we read
the following words about him: "So God remembered Abraham and
sent Lot out of the midst of the overthrow." So it was not quite in vain
when Abraham pleaded for Sodom. And this points us to the one who
threw himself into the breach for our Sodom. He intercedes with God
for us and for all the inhabitants of Sodom. And he pleads with us to
depart from Sodom. It is an unpopular demand, and yet it is vitally
necessary.

But our great hope in Christ hinders us from pushing aside the things
that he requires of us. For this hope requires of us a departure and a
separation that are no less clear and unambiguous than the one the
messengers required of Lot. As long as we are on the road between
Sodom and Zoar, Jesus will keep us moving, so that everyone does what
is the right thing—the right thing for him. What does he call to us in the
Gospel of Luke (17:31–33)? "Let him who is in the field not turn back to
what is behind him. Remember Lot's wife. Whoever seeks to gain his life
will lose it, but whoever loses his life will preserve it."

Filming has begun for the feature "Sodom and Gomorrah." We are the actors, whether we like it or not. But we still have the chance to change over to a better role. And so, the peace of God, which passes all understanding, keep your hearts and minds in Christ Jesus.

Lord, what is going to happen to Lot's wife? Does the pillar of salt have to go on standing where it stands now? Grant her a warm, reviving bath! Have mercy on all the petrified lives among us.

Lord, did you not go into the realm of the dead for Lot's sons-in-law too? Look upon all those who find your word an absurdity. Lead them into the right way, before their laughter dies away on their lips.

Lord, do you not see Lot in the midst of us? Do you see how he lingers, how quickly he grows tired? You have often sent us your messengers before. The word is not enough. We need their hands to pull us out of the danger zones. Make your messengers our best friends. You expect us to climb steep mountains. Have mercy on our weakness even if we only get as far as Zoar.

Lord, do not let your messengers die out. Send them out from among us as well, two by two. Courageous messengers, who do not conceal the hour that has struck. Energetic messengers, who lend a helping hand to the people who linger on the way to liberty. Here is the money we have collected. Use it for the real benefit of these young offenders. Give their pastor your authority as your own messenger.

Lord, with Abraham we plead for the whole of Sodom and Gomorrah. For Jesus' sake, we entreat you for Sodom and Gomorrah in all the countries of our world, in the divisions of the United Nations, in our country, in our university, in the personal lives of us all. In Jesus' name we beseech you, as he has taught us: Our Father . . .

3

Stop!

Sermon on Exodus 34:21a*

Let the peace of Christ rule in our hearts, to which indeed we are called. Amen.

Listen to the commandment about the day of rest, as we find it in Exod. 34:21a:

> Six days you shall work, but on the seventh day you shall stop working.

Lord, shed your influence upon us anew today, and say to each one of us, "Let there be light!" so that all darkness may depart from us. Amen.

What we have just heard is the tersest, and probably the oldest, form of the commandment about the day of rest. There are many other versions in the Old Testament as well, with detailed explanations and comments. In the framework of the Ten Commandments, this one is more fully elaborated than any of the others. Apparently no other commandment for practical living is thought to have so fundamental and far-reaching an importance as just this call to put work aside every seventh day, to interrupt all business for one whole day in the week. Indeed, this is really a call for a regularly repeated, demonstrative strike against all the importunate employers round about us and in ourselves.

Why is this commandment in particular stressed so emphatically? (Incidentally, apart from the commandment to honor one's parents, it is the only one framed in positive terms.) We discover the answer if we go on to ask: what recurs in all the different versions of the commandment? There is only one thing: on the seventh day you are to lay your

---

*Preached in the university service in the Peterskirche, Heidelberg, on Cantate Sunday, May 9, 1971.

work aside. It is this that makes it especially evident that the command-ments are real blessings—like some pleasant and effective prescription the doctor gives us: you are not to do anything on the seventh day, and you can have a completely clear conscience into the bargain! You are to be a lazybones, by order! This is the voice of mercy, the voice of liberty. Anyone who has perhaps not perceived this truth in the other com-mandments cannot fail to notice it here, once and for all. If it were not this voice of liberty, this merciful invitation, it surely wouldn't be God's holy law, it wouldn't be the holy law of the God of the Bible, the holy law of the Father of Jesus Christ. The God who encounters us in the com-mandment about the day of rest is not—as Martin Buber once said—aiming to hand out medals or prison cells at some later point. With his commandment and in his commandment he is giving us honor and liberty—the honor of free human beings who can regularly allow them-selves a completely free day. This is what the commandment about the day of rest emphasizes more than anything else—though in the other commandments, too, the things we are required to leave undone are far more than the things we are required to perform.

What do we do with this offer? Isn't our seventh day largely a devasta-tion, or at least threatened on every side? There have been state laws enjoining Sunday observance ever since Constantine issued the first one in A.D. 321, but they have hardly been able to prevent the havoc. Academics fall on the "day of rest" eagerly, so that the rattle of their typewriters and the rustle of the pages of their prescribed reading are more continuous on Sunday than on any other day of the week. Other people let themselves be sucked into the vortex of the recreation indus-try and are no less nerve-rackingly busy with their hobbies than they are with their jobs. A third group of people protests against the bourgeois Sunday as a shabby trick on the part of the exploiters, who are only aiming to breed a more productive work force and want to keep them in a good humor; for people like this, Sunday is a working day when they can deliberately implement their plans. In the old days Israel was proba-bly familiar with just as many similar threats. At all events, the Sabbath Commandment had to be continually reemphasized.

So let us ask quite precisely: what is the point of this strict order to lay down our work? I deduce the answers from the different forms that the commandment about the day of rest takes. I hope I can say what I want to say, and I hope you can listen to it, in such a way that we shall gladly think of it on all the Sundays ahead. As far as I can see, the Old Testament commandment about the day of rest gives us five answers to the question *why*.

1. It wants to remind us of freedom conferred. That is why we can read in Deut. 5:15: "Remember that you were a slave in the land of Egypt, and the Lord your God brought you out thence with a mighty hand and an outstretched arm; therefore the Lord your God commanded you to keep the sabbath day." Both for Israel and for us this means: remember that a liberator is at work on your behalf, someone who is able to cope with all the slaveowners and with the powerful people who put upon you. But it is someone who can cope too with everything you load on to yourself, with your self-tormenting, compulsive industry, and with your indefatigable pursuit of hobbies and recreation which, if they begin to become your master, can make you yourself and other people just as unhappy. Christians started to celebrate the first day of the week as the day of Jesus' resurrection (Matt. 28:1), as "the Lord's day" (Rev. 1:10). Ever since that time, every seventh day is supposed to be a vivid reminder to people that now our liberator is unconquerable by any power or any death. When we lay down our work we can remind ourselves and other people that God himself has taken our cause into his own hands, in mercy and in power. Jesus lives for us, the Jesus who on his way to the cross practiced forgiveness instead of retaliation. We are all fully accepted by God just as we are, ahead of all our "performance" and before we achieve anything at all. So we must not allow our failings to accuse us; the things half-done and the fragments of our work which we left unfinished at the end of the week must not trouble us:

> My own good works all came to naught,
> No grace or merit gaining.

But:

> To me he said: "Stay close to me;
> I am your rock and castle.
> Your ransom I myself will be,
> For you I'll strive and wrestle.

> For I am yours and you are mine,
> And where I am you may remain.
> The foe shall not divide us."

Even all the confusion in the world must not make too great an impression on us. What *is* supposed to impress us, and what we are supposed to be newly aware of every Sunday, is the fact that the liberator of us all is the only One who has death behind him. Ever since Easter, Christians have gathered together on the first day of the week. The Book of Acts (20:7–12) tells us about the congregation in Troas, who met to break bread and to listen. That is to say, they met to celebrate the feast marking the bond of love with their living Lord and with one another; and they met to listen. On the first day of the week they had time to listen— plenty of time. Paul talked and talked and talked until midnight, so that one man fell out of the window (though he didn't die of it after all); and afterward Paul went on talking and talking until the sun rose on the day when he left. So Christians celebrate this day with the breaking of bread and in listening. Without meeting together like this in some way or other, it is probably impossible for people to escape from their endless rotating around themselves and their own doings. We are so restless that we can probably only come to a halt if we listen to the One who mediates the liberty we have been given. Calvin said we should stop working so that God could work in us. But the reverse is true as well. It is when God works in us, and only then, that we find peace and come to ourselves. Are we really seriously in danger today of being legalistic in our sanctification of the day of rest? This fear is not so important for us nowadays as the need to lay our work aside as a clear demonstration that "For freedom Christ has set you free; do not submit any more to a yoke of slavery!" (Gal. 5:1). We need a regular reminder of the great freedom that has already been conferred on us. Once a week at least, this should make us laugh, as we remember that all the things which are the bane of our lives are going to die one day, while the love and supremacy of our liberator is final.

Let us go on to ask further about the special point of the command to lay aside our work. It is surely not designed merely to free us for worship.

2. It is intended to make us free to rejoice in creation. In the Ten Commandments, in the form in which we know them from Exodus 20, the reason given for the Sabbath Commandment is this: "In six days the Lord made heaven and earth, the sea, and all that is in them, and rested the seventh day; therefore the Lord blessed the sabbath day and hallowed it." "He blessed it." That means, he provided it with special powers. "He hallowed it." That is to say, he kept it in quite a different way from all the other days. This reminds human beings that they have been put into a finished world which is supplied with everything necessary and with many, many other things that are simply pleasurable and lovely. The first creation account describes in a splendid way how the first day of man's life was immediately his first great day of rest, after the six days of God's creation. It was a day of joy over everything that had been created for him. So Christians have done rightly in not wanting to *close* the week with rest but in celebrating *the first* day of the week as a rest day. From this starting point we should descend cheerfully into the week, not climb steeply upwards. Our work can then acquire more of the character of play. It can become, too, something of a protest against the principle of performance and the pressure to produce results. For everything we need for living has long since been given—this is what the first creation account reminds us of—though our perceptions are often too dull for us to grasp the fact. All we have to do is to harvest properly what the Creator has bestowed on us. We have our hands full with seeing to it that we do not spoil it all and make a mess of what we have been given. The first day is there above all else to waken our joy in creation. This is essential for our attitude to life as a whole. Without the work of God that preceded us, human beings are not conceivable at all. But if in spite of that a person tries to think of himself without God, life becomes meaningless. It crumbles away in his hands. And then he can find neither a proper relationship to work nor to rest. We then ask tensely what we are there for, and why the world is there. But there is no utilitarian reason why anything should exist at all, as Jürgen Moltmann says. The Bible explains to us why creation took place. The Wisdom that was present during God's creative act says: "Then I was daily his delight, playing before him always" (Prov. 8:30). Sunday wants to pass on this joy in the play of creation. We are permit-

ted to enter into a wide space prepared for us by God, out and away from our stuffy confines.

This means quite specifically: we are allowed to let our joy well up over the exuberant luxury of types and colors, and the lavish and motley wealth of life. We are permitted to rejoice because—in the words of a contemporary biologist—"the birds sing far more than they have any right to do, according to Darwin." Little groups ought to organize wildcat strikes against our overorganized Sundays. They should rush out and rediscover all the treasures of the countryside that lies at our back door, with all its birds and beasts and flowers. We don't need to go far afield. We can begin to play again, and to swim, and to dance. For when we play the loser wins too. To be able to spend the holiday like this is simply a delight in itself. Even Calvin, strict as he was, permitted a game of boccie on Sunday afternoons, to the glory of God. Instead of going on with our fanatical discussions, which we pursue so inexorably and with such austere rigidity, we can spend our afternoon walk telling jokes and exchanging stories. I learnt this week that even in the period of dry-as-dust orthodoxy, Easter sermons often began with a joke. *Risus paschalis* was the name given to the Easter laughter which is appropriate for the Lord's day. Perhaps some of us will even begin to sing, or play an instrument again, as a way of practicing our joy over our liberty. For that is the point of our having a *common* day of rest: to share our joys and to find joy in one another—to rejoice together over creation.

So this is the second reason for the day of rest. We heard that the day of rest reminds us first of all of the liberty we have been given; now we hear that it also makes us free for joy in creation.

But how can we play and sing and rejoice with any conscience when for so many people the world is a hell—in Pakistan, in Vietnam, in Jordan, and here at home too? What does the commandment about the day of rest ask of us here?

3. It encourages us to bring help to the specially burdened. These people find special mention in the more extended versions of the Sabbath Commandment, in the context of the Ten Commandments. In Exod. 20:10 we are told: "You shall not do any work, you, or your son, or your daughter, your manservant, or your maidservant, or your cattle, or the sojourner who is within your gates." The parallel version (Deut. 5:14) adds: ". . . that your manservant and your maidservant may rest as

well as you." The Sabbath begins with equality. On this day at least parents should stop dealing out orders to their sons and daughters, let alone to their subordinates. In an early version, in the Book of the Covenant (Exod. 23:12), the whole commandment is actually formulated in such a way that its sole point is the overburdened and their lot. The passage runs: "Six days you shall do your work, but on the seventh day you shall rest; that your ox and your ass may have rest, and the son of your bondmaid [he was the ultimate dependent who in borderline cases could always be forced to work], and the alien [like the slaves] may be refreshed." Here the commandment is concerned initially with the overburdened close at hand. In one of the few passages in the New Testament in which the first day of the week is mentioned—at the end of the First Epistle to the Corinthians (16:2)—this day was to be used to gather money and put it aside for the people in Jerusalem who were in need.

Which of us would ever remember Release Heidelberg [a rehabilitation center for drug addicts—trans.] if we were not reminded of it on the day of rest? Who would think about our congregation's responsibility in India if this were not brought to our attention on Sunday? Our collection today is for our India program. We still lack the money we require to help our needy friends in India and their work. Today is the last collection which can be used for this purpose during this summer term. The men and women in Corinth were supposed to think of the saints in Jerusalem. Let us give a firm helping hand to our friends in India! For the day of rest has been given us for the sake of people who are harassed and overburdened, so that we may help them. Let us make these people a really large donation, out of joy over the liberty we have been given.

Strangers far away from us are pushed out of our egoistical working days. But in the peace of God's presence they should come close to us, so that our self-seeking, closed-in social order is given a new form which reaches out to them too. The strangers in our city should be given a share in our joy over our liberty as well. When otherwise do we have so much time for invitations—free time that is actually prescribed for us— so that strangers can find refreshment in our houses or our gardens? And then, not least, we are commanded to rest for the sake of people round about who are sick, or lonely, or depressed. In whatever guise we encounter these slaves of our modern world, on the day of rest we are at last free for a conversation that is more than mere surface talk. We can write more than a postcard to people who have long been waiting to hear from us. " 'He had time for me.' You will hardly be given any greater testimony than that before the throne of God," wrote Ludwig Köhler once. "He had time for me." If only everything flows from our joy over the freedom we have been given and the assurance that nothing can separate us from the love of God. For Jesus impresses on us that the Sabbath is made for man and not man for the Sabbath (Mark 2:27). The Sabbath shouldn't turn into a kind of sanctimonious bustle. On this day nothing must degenerate into work. But a sanctimonious, legalistic idleness is rejected too. How much time we gain if, after six days, we really let our work alone for one full, complete day—our work and our obsessive pursuit of recreation too.

This is the third thing we should notice. First, the day of rest is to remind us of liberty conferred; second, it should free us for joy in creation; third, it should make it possible for people who are specially burdened to find refreshment with us. It is probably because of this third point that the commandment about the day of rest is impressed on us so seriously, as we shall see.

4. It aims to impress on us the senselessness of incessant work. The manna story in Exodus 16 tells us this in an almost humorous way. Every day fresh bread fell from heaven; every day in the week it had to be collected afresh. The bread from the day before was rotten. But on the sixth day a double amount fell from heaven. What was intended for the seventh day "did not become foul, and there were no worms in it," we are told (vv. 22–24). But of course there were some people who couldn't restrain themselves—just like people today—from going out to gather the manna on the seventh day too—"and they found none" (v. 27). So bustling activity on the seventh day is mocked at, as a slight to God's providing care, and as quite simply futile. The prophet Amos (8:5) condemns the corn merchants who couldn't wait for the Sabbath to end, so that they could sell corn again and cheat people with poor wares, false weights and exorbitant prices. The early text which we read at the beginning (Exod. 34:21a) has been expanded. We heard: "Six days you shall work, but on the seventh day you shall rest." And then a phrase was added: "even in ploughing time and in harvest."

Then, especially, just when work is particularly pressing and is mounting up—that is the time when a person needs the day of rest. When the addition was made the Holy Spirit was probably thinking about the time when people are finishing their seminar papers and working for their exams. Or he had us teachers in mind, too, with the accumulation of meetings and lectures, which have to be coped with in addition to the usual week's work, and which demand the utmost of us. A vintner who has his vineyard just outside the city told me recently: "I've often found that someone who doesn't keep Sunday is sometime or other given time during the week to make up for it. Many a one who thinks he always has to work in his strawberry fields on Sunday too—strawberries do well out here; you can do good business with them—has to make the time up in weeks of illness." That was what this simple vintner told me. I find a remarkable provision in the Old Testament: Israel was actually supposed to grant her land complete Sabbath rest every seventh year (Lev. 25:2–7). We are then told that the period of exile was meant to repay the land for the sabbatical years that had been neglected (Lev. 26:43). A wise old rule says: "If you are particularly hurried, sit down first and do nothing at all; things will work out just as well."

A day of rest shared gives double rest. It is only if we are brave enough to make a pause that our work retains something of the splendor of the liberty given to the redeemed and something of the joy of creation. It is only in this way that we come to ourselves and arrive at what gives our whole life meaning. Karl Barth once asked: "Can one understand the working day unless one has understood the day of rest first?"—he meant as the prolongation of freedom conferred and as another way of rejoicing over creation.

We have now gathered together four insights: the commandment about the day of rest wants to remind us of liberty conferred; to free us for joy in creation; to give refreshment, through our help, to people who are specially burdened; and to emphasize the senselessness of incessant work. But we are all aware in practical terms of the opposition—indeed the conflict— between our workload and the holiday. It is a conflict we often find crushing; and this may make some of us perhaps feel restive now. In spite of all the repeated attempts of faith, it is still a conflict we find difficult to resolve. And for that reason we should think about yet another, final meaning of the day of rest.

5. It is designed to be a prelude to the liberty that will be final and complete, and to be an intimation of that liberty. In the Epistle to the Colossians (2:16–17, altered) we read that Sabbaths are to be understood as "a shadow of what is to come, which has become substance in Christ." In the period of the exile, in Babylonia, Israel was very specially oppressed in the foreign land to which it had been banished. And then the day of rest, which was unknown in the world around, became the token of the covenant, the sign of Israel's faith. The prophet Ezekiel says: "You shall hallow my sabbaths that they may be a sign between me and you, that you may know that I the Lord am your God" (Ezek. 20:20). This meant a great deal in that era of oppression. In Exod. 31:12–17, the person who breaks the Sabbath is threatened with the death penalty, unbelievable though this seems to us today. And yet no particular "performance" is demanded, not even the requirement to take part in worship. All we are asked to do is—nothing. We are told to rest. In this way Israel was supposed to demonstrate that it lived solely from the works of God. The Sabbath was thus supposed to be the pledge of the eternal covenant, a permanent sign for a people who had been given freedom in hope. In our meritocracy, people proudly proclaim even in obituary notices: "His life was work." God's people had to learn the very opposite: anyone who cannot rest and be quiet is already the victim of death.

The day of rest is intended to be the prelude to final liberty, an eschatological event in the midst of our provisional existence, a sign of what is ultimate. This is brought out in two ways. First of all, the seventh day is supposed to be a continual inspiration to finding new and freer molds for the whole week. It has already done this, directly or indirectly, in the course of the centuries. It is supposed to be the day that provides the norm, the pattern for the others, the day when we really come to life again. What we should really find desirable is the actual reversal of our meritocracy's slogan "His life was work." His life was rest—his life was freedom—his life was joy, and that included his work too. That would be true praise, if someone could say that about our weeks. Sunday's leisure can make us inventive about finding ways to give a freer form to the week's work too. And yet even this, just by itself, would still be much too little, because it still belongs within the framework of the world of death.

But the day of rest is above all a sign of hope for the full liberty of the children of God for which the whole troubled creation waits. Every Sunday, as the first day of the week, reminds us of the creation of light and above all of the raising of Jesus from the dead, as pledge of the resurrection of all, as pledge of the new world which God has promised us. In the same way, every day of rest is permitted to be a little prelude and allusion to the new humanity in which every tear will be wiped away and when there will be no more death and no more suffering, when no more crying will be heard, and when there will be no more pain to be endured (Rev. 21:4). After all, Christians already mock and deride death in their Easter and Sunday hymns: "Where, O death, is now thy sting? Where thy victory, O grave?" Psalm 126 is already an overture: "Then our mouth shall be filled with laughter. The Lord has done great things for us; whereof we are glad." Every first day of the week ought to remind each one of us of "the Last Days." We should remember that we are making much too little out of Sunday if it does not remind us—at least as a far-off echo—of the day of full and utter liberty. In this light, a new generation could once again enjoy making Sunday a somewhat more festal occasion, from the breakfast table on. But in view of the perfected day to which this points, the really important thing is more merriment. "A glad heart makes a cheerful countenance" (Prov. 15:13). We should put more brightness into Sunday.

In these new times the congregation must develop new customs, for itself and in the community as a whole, so that the world around grasps more about our present realization of the liberty we have been given, our joy in creation, the help ready for the specially burdened, the senselessness of incessant work, and this prelude to ultimate and complete liberty. Each of us might think about this, and talk to one another about ways in which, from now on, we should change our attitude to the seventh day (as the first day), and our practical behavior as well. For we and our world are truly permitted to enjoy the blessing of God's commandment: "Six days you shall work, but on the seventh day you shall rest, even in ploughing time and in harvest." Amen.

> We thank you, O Lord our God, for your clear and goodly commandment.
> We do not find it easy to accept as the help you are giving us for our own time.

Help each one of us to lay his work aside and to celebrate Sunday with new joy.

You free us from the burden of our past.

Take into your own hands the fragments of the work we have done during the past week.

Open our eyes and ears today for your creation.

You give us time for the people who are specially burdened.

Help us to find the way to ourselves. We are incorrigible, and yet you permit us to taste already the feast of perfect freedom.

Have mercy on your Christians, who talk about you, but without doing your will.

Help your church to live more fully in the joy you have brought about.

Give it many people who will help to discover happy ways of celebrating Sunday together, in large and small groups and communities—artists and doctors, biologists and technicians, sociologists, teachers and pastors, good speakers, musicians and organizers, on radio and television as well.

We pray for all the people who have to work on Sunday. Let them meet with gratitude, recognition, and help, and sometimes find someone who will stand in for them. And let them be given a full equivalent during the week.

We pray for the very lonely, for the sick, for the dying, for families and neighbors who have quarrelled, for people who are depressed and troubled in mind, for the overburdened. We pray for the despairing who seek an escape in alcohol or drugs. Equip men and women in your church on Sunday who can stand by them with the power of your love.

Give our families and the communities in which we live the tranquillity and repose to make real understanding possible. Give us pleasure in playing together. Let those who bear the chief burden of the household during the week be given a real respite on Sunday.

And all this to the praise of thy love. Amen.

4

The Essential Prayer

Sermon on 1 Kings 3:5–15*

At Gibeon the Lord appeared to Solomon in a dream by night; and God said, "Ask what I shall give you." And Solomon said, "Thou hast shown great and steadfast love to thy servant David my father, because he walked before thee in faithfulness, in righteousness, and in uprightness of heart toward thee; and thou hast kept for him this great and steadfast love, and hast given him a son to sit on his throne this day. And now, O Lord my God, thou hast made thy servant king in place of David my father, although I am but young; I do not know how to go out or come in. And thy servant is in the midst of thy people whom thou hast chosen, a great people, that cannot be numbered or counted for multitude. Give thy servant therefore an obedient heart to govern thy people, that I may discern between good and evil; for who is able to govern this thy great people?"

It pleased the Lord that Solomon had asked this. And God said to him, "Because you have asked this, and have not asked for yourself long life or riches or the life of your enemies, but have asked for yourself understanding to hear and to judge rightly, behold, I now do according to your word. Behold, I give you a wise and discerning heart, so that none like you has been before you and none like you shall arise after you. I give you also what you have not asked, both riches and honor, so that no other king shall compare with you, all your days. And if you will walk in my ways, keeping my statutes and my commandments, as your father David walked, then I will lengthen your days."

And Solomon awoke, and behold, it was a dream. Then he came to Jerusalem, and stood before the ark of the covenant of the Lord, and offered up burnt offerings and peace offerings, and made a feast for all his servants.

This text asks us what we expect for ourselves from our petitions. In the middle of the passage we are told: "It pleased the Lord that Solo-

---

*Sermon preached to theology students at a midweek service in the theological seminary in Wuppertal on the Wednesday before Rogate Sunday, 1955.

mon had asked this." Can we put our prayers beside this one? Perhaps our prayer this morning?

We know that the right to pray is our privilege: "Ask what I shall give you." This unbelievable privilege, which is granted to King Solomon here, is given to us all through Jesus Christ: "If you ask anything of the Father in my name, he will give it to you." In saying this Jesus put us side by side with the Old Testament king.

Are we really aware what a tremendous privilege this is? It often doesn't seem like it. It must be said that among theologians prayer plays a lamentable role. When we are supposed to pray, the reaction is often painful embarrassment. God stands there with full hands—"Ask what I shall give you"—and we are agonizingly concerned with ourselves. And yet it is prayer that decides whether we are theologians—or historians whose special subject is the history of religion, or philosophers specializing in metaphysics. It is prayer that decides whether the subject of our studies is a present, living subject. The royal privilege is conferred on us again today.

But then comes the real question: the question about the content of our prayers. What are the things for which we solicit God's attention? Why and when do we call on his help? Let us compare our prayer with Solomon's. What kind of prayer was it that pleased God?

We see first of all that the prayer has an introduction, an approach—a rather long one, in fact. The actual petition itself is then very brief. So the prelude is evidently important. Every real prayer needs an approach of this kind. Otherwise we remain within ourselves. Before anything else, Solomon expresses his sense of what God has done. He thinks of the mercy that God showed his father David, and the fact that he is now allowed to sit on David's throne. Recollections like this of what God has done give us courage to ask. If you are despondent and fainthearted, think first of all about what God has done for you. Begin with Christ's birth, or with the first call of Jesus you ever heard, and end up in gratitude at the point you have reached today, the point to which he has brought you. The remembrance of God's faithfulness and his activity on our behalf draws us once more into the great onward movement of God's history, and takes away the weariness and somnolence of people who simply mark time when they are praying—and at other times too. But this is not the end of the prelude to Solomon's petition.

In the second part Solomon thinks of the tremendous tasks confronting him as king over a people which is not only large, but which God has also chosen—which therefore means a people for whom God has a special purpose. In the face of this task he is frightened by his own youthfulness. He doesn't know where to turn. This forces him to pray. Any one of us who takes a proper view of the task in front of him today has no choice either but to make his way to God. God has thought out a task for us all, something we have to do among the people for whom he has his great plan; and again and again we see that we cannot even cope with ourselves. Anyone whom this reduces to complete despondency perceives with special clarity that he cannot let God's great offer slip by unused: "Ask what I shall give you."

This is the prelude to the prayer: a recollection of God's acts and the tasks he is giving us. Anyone who begins to pray sees himself first of all as the creature of God's unremitting faithfulness, and second as an inefficient tool whom God wants to use for new acts. The first recognition gives us the courage to pray. The second forces us to pray.

Now, after this long prelude, comes the short petition: give me an obedient heart—a hearing heart. That is the whole content of the prayer. That is all. This is the essential prayer. It is the Gethsemane prayer: "Not as I will, but as thou wilt." It is the prayer that is entirely attuned to what God has to say. It begins when we surrender ourselves into God's hand. And that is where it ends. It is a subordination to what God does and what he intends. That is why the heart wants to hear. That is why we want to hear *with our hearts*; for that means drawing the necessary conclusions. But none of us has this hearing heart. And yet it is the one thing we absolutely need if we are to remain—or if we are to become—God's creatures and his instruments. Otherwise we are crushed by a catalogue of duties, the expectations of the people around us, our own program, the tremendous task which no one less than God has assigned to us and which we cannot therefore simply put aside. Otherwise we are crushed by the fear of our own weakness, lack of independence, faintheartedness—the fear of ourselves, as we are. Only a hearing heart could free us from this terrible dilemma. If only we had it!

We do not have it. But we can ask for it. That is the prayer which pleases God. It isn't easy to let all other petitions go, for the sake of this one prayer. It can cost us many a struggle with ourselves. We can escape from our twistings and turnings only if we remember what God has done for us and what the tasks are which he has in mind for us. We remain perverted and warped until this is the sole substance of our prayer: give me a hearing heart!

God was pleased that Solomon had not asked for a long life. That request is a very modern one: give me more time! But we do not need more time. What we need is a hearing heart which uses the hours and days in obedience. We only lack time because we lack a hearing heart. God has only one particular assignment for each particular hour. If our hearts hear, then the time is filled—and fulfilled. God waits today for men and women who come out of the hurry and the rush and ask of him fulfilled time. He wants people who are not ambitious to keep up with the contemporary rat race, but whose aim is to maintain contact with him.

It pleased God that Solomon did not ask for riches. This request is just as modern as the first. Give me security! But we do not need any more security for our existence. What we need is a hearing heart which uses the opportunities we are given—and those we are refused—in obedience. We are only out for a higher standard of living because we lack a hearing heart. That is the only reason we suffer over not having enough. But God's plans with Lazarus in his poverty are no less important than his plans with Dives in his wealth. If we have a hearing heart we shall have a fulfilled life, in riches and in poverty. Today God is waiting for men and women who will break away from their profit-seeking and whose whole wealth is his Word.

It pleased God that Solomon did not ask for the souls of his enemies. This petition is dangerously familiar. It is the request to be one of the victors in this world, not one of the defeated; to be successful, to be able to play the important role; it is a prayer not to be one of the people who don't make the grade. But what we all need is not more success, but a hearing heart, which in obedience contents itself with the position God has given us. We are only ambitious or dejected because we lack a hearing heart. But God has his particular charge for the winners and for the defeated, for the successful and for the failures, for the first and for the last. The first will be last, and the One who was crucified is the Lord of all. God waits today for men and women to escape from their overweening arrogance and from their inferiority complexes. He waits for people who are prepared to ask that they may respond to the place he has given them with a grateful yes. He waits for people who do not assess their lives against the lives of other people, but who test them against what God's goodness says. Solomon was a king. He asked for a hearing heart so that he might "govern God's people and discern between good and evil. For who is able to govern this thy great people?" He needs a hearing heart because he has to be responsible for other people, for God's people. Anyone who is supposed to guide other people requires a hearing heart most of all. Otherwise he will be a tyrant or a fool, but not God's instrument in the midst of his people. We can only be preachers and pastors if we have hearing hearts. But which of us does not have tasks to perform for other people? We must all realize that the plea for the obedient heart covers my particular service among the people round about me, who are also God's people.

Let us sum up. We are faced today with the question about the content of our prayers and petitions. Every true prayer is a kind of exorcism which drives out all other petitions through the one plea: give me a hearing heart to discern and carry out what you want me to do among my fellow human beings. This is the petition for every day. It is born out of gratitude for what God has done, and out of a sense of our own guilt.

Let me close with two questions.

1. Do we also wait for God's answer to our request? God says to Solomon: "Because you have asked this and nothing else, I will give it to you. And by doing so I will mark you out among all other people. And I will give you many, many other reasons for thankfulness in addition." Not everyone in the Old Testament receives an answer to his petitions. Occasionally someone has to get up without an answer to his prayer, and has to wait for days before he receives that answer; but not forever.

Through Jesus Christ, this has changed. In him we can find God's answer to our prayer every day. With his Spirit he sees to it that every day our hearts have something to hear, and that they are able to discern what that message is. All we have to do is to ask him and to wait for an answer. It is clear that the request for a hearing heart is a request made before the open Bible. It is clear that it is only a right prayer if it waits for what God has to say. Do we wait for the answer to our request which God gives us with Jesus Christ? Do we hear how he wants to fill our hours, how he wants the gifts he has given us to be actively used, and what ministry he wants from us for the benefit of his people? If we do pray at all, our prayer usually suffers because we break off too soon. So we should think about the question: do we wait for God's response? The "Amen" belongs at the end of the word God speaks to us.

2. What do we do when our prayer has ended? Does our day go on in the usual way, just as if nothing had happened? Solomon did two things. First of all he made a thank-offering in Jerusalem before the Ark of the Lord; and then he held a great feast for all his servants. Every right prayer which has heard God's response flowers into these same two things: new gratitude and new love. One of the sacrifices of joy is the broken and fearful heart which we are permitted to give up. The keynote is joy. We have won time to sing songs of thanksgiving to God. Then there is the feast for the servants. The people who are close to someone who prays are well-off. Our seminary, our student community, does not live from rules and regulations, or from rights and duties. It lives from people who pray. For they have time and strength for the people round them. So this is the second question which we should take with us to think about: what do we do after we have prayed? Amen.

5

Someone in Despair

Sermon on the 73d Psalm*

May the peace of God reign in our hearts. Amen.
We shall read from the 73d Psalm, initially the first two verses only:

> In spite of everything,
> God is good to the upright,
>   to those who are pure in heart.
> But as for me, my feet had almost stumbled,
> my steps had well-nigh slipped.

Lord, send forth your light and your truth that they may lead us.
Amen.

What a tense situation this is into which the psalmist draws us with his
very first sentence. It is the tension between belief and unbelief, between doubt and certainty, between standing and falling. As far as he
himself is concerned, he admits without any reserve: I wasn't merely
very uncertain—I had almost lost my faith altogether. I was really at the
very point when doubt could easily have sent me headlong.

But before he tells us this about himself, and some other things as
well, the psalmist has something general to say about the whole situation. And this is what he begins with, in his first sentence: "In spite of
everything God is Israel's consolation. God is good for people who are
upright—in spite of everything." For the man who is writing, this is anything but a matter of course. His opening sentence anticipates the final
result of a long history of personal uncertainty. He is going to explain it
all to us in what follows. He evidently thinks that what he has experi-

---

*Preached in the university service in the Peterskirche, Heidelberg, on Rogate Sunday,
May 27, 1973.

enced can be of vital importance for other people too; and he wants to let them share his discovery that "God is good to the upright."

So let us see what this unfamiliar voice has to tell us. In the lines that follow he will answer the questions that his first sentences raise in our minds. First of all, what brought him within a hair's breadth of losing his faith? Second, how did he get through the crisis in his life? Third, what kind of person, then, can expect to experience God's goodness, in spite of everything?

The psalmist answers the first of these questions immediately, and in some detail: what almost made him stumble? Let us read vv. 3–12:

> For I was envious of the boastful,
>   when I saw the prosperity of the godless.
> For they go through no agonies,
>   their bellies are full and sleek.
> They are not in trouble as other people are;
>   they are not stricken like others.
> Therefore they preen themselves in their arrogance,
>   the garment of violence wraps them round.
> Their eyes swell out with fatness,
>   and their hearts overflow with follies.
> They are engrossed in malignancy and speak with malice;
>   loftily they threaten oppression.
> They open their mouths as wide as to the heavens,
>   and their tongue struts through the earth.
>   [What a hint for a caricaturist!—au.]
> Therefore the people run after them.
>   They greedily gobble up their words.
> And they say, "What can God know?
>   Is there knowledge in the Most Highest?"
> Just so are the godless:
>   always at ease, they increase in power.

These successful people have therefore robbed our psalmist of his self-confidence. It was not intellectual difficulties which made him stumble, and not direct attacks either. It was a whole series of silent observations of his own, of the kind which had already forced Jeremiah to ask: "Why does the way of the wicked prosper? Why do all who are treacherous thrive?" (Jer. 12:1). He is on his own, confronted by a whole series of other people who are bursting with health and who give free rein to all their desires. Everything works out well for them. They know how to get their way with other people, either by deceit or through violence. They are like the monster out of Chaos which an ancient Canaanite text from Ugarit describes: "One lip in heaven, the other on earth, his tongue plays on the stars." These are not criminal types on the fringes of society. They belong to the elite and the powerful. They impress the rank and file. Their tongues can utter brutal threats just as easily as bright nothings. They don't even find God worth hostility. At most he rates a witty question in passing—a remark that puts him down as of no interest. They achieve all the glittering prizes life has to offer, completely without God. Do they not continually reap the blessing which earlier generations believed God reserved for the devout? These are the kind of questions the psalmist must have asked. And what are our questions? Don't science, economics, and politics get along better than ever, without God? Isn't your atheist neighbor happier than you? Why do 90 percent of our people boycott sermons altogether? Isn't the isolated psalmist's question about God hollow and pointless? Even senseless self-torment?

What does he think about himself? Let us read on, in vv. 13–16:

> All in vain have I kept my heart clean
> and washed my hands in innocence.
> For all the day long I have been stricken,
> and chastened every morning.
> If I had said, "I will speak like them,"
> at that moment I would have betrayed the life of thy sons.
> I thought and thought how I should understand these things—
> it was a torment to me.

Which of us does not know something of these temptations? We realize now how little a matter of course the first sentence of the psalm is—and how unacceptable at first: "God is good to the upright." And we realize too how indispensable at least the phrase that precedes that assertion is—the "in spite of everything." This "pure heart" was the very opposite of a simple-minded, naive piety. The psalmist no longer saw any point in tormenting himself morally and intellectually. Even physically he is on the borderline of what is endurable. Has he not far more reason than those fortunate "wicked" simply to smile derisively at the word "God"?

47

Only one thing keeps him from it: the thought of people whom he calls "God's sons." He would have betrayed them if he had lightly given God up. Perhaps he is thinking of the much-tested Abraham or the much-tempted Job. Who are the witnesses to the faith, in past and present, that prevent us from an over-hasty move into the camp of the godless? Who are the people to whom we cannot avoid paying silent respect? Perhaps Blaise Pascal? Perhaps Dietrich Bonhoeffer? Perhaps the person who helped us to find faith? Perhaps it is only one person, Jesus of Nazareth himself, *the* Son of God. Do these people hold us back? Perhaps. God cannot simply be dismissed with a wave of the hand. The remembrance of people whom we cannot overlook fortunately still acts as a brake when we are already racing down the slippery slope. But this only prolongs the torment of thinking and comparing: why are the godless so happy? Other, later poets have expressed for us what this torment of the mind can be like:

> O the mind, mind has mountains; cliffs of fall
> Frightful, sheer, no-man-fathomed. Hold them cheap
> May who ne'er hung there.
>> (Gerard Manley Hopkins,
>> "No Worst, There Is None")

Which of us may perhaps say like the psalmist: "I thought and thought how I should understand these things—it was a torment to me"? Who doesn't rub himself raw somewhere or other? Who is not aware of his inadequacies? But it is just at this very point that we come face to face with the decisive turning point in our psalm. Let us look on to vv. 17–22:

> Until I went into the sanctuary of God;
>> then I perceived their end. ·
> Truly thou dost set them in slippery places;
>> thou lettest them fall into delusions.
> How they collapse in a moment!
>> They end, they disappear with terrors.
> They are like a dream when one awakes, Lord,
>> so is their image despised in the city.
> When my soul was embittered,
>> and my heart deeply wounded,
> Then I was like a beast without understanding,
>> like an ox I stood before thee.

So now the psalmist answers our second question: how did he find his way out of this profound crisis? It lasted only until he "went into the sanctuary of God." If we are to come to terms with our own questions, everything now depends on our grasping what this "going into the sanctuary" means. The psalmist is describing a change of place. He doesn't insist on sticking to his own old standpoint, where he searches heaven and earth in vain for a meaning and then fights the endless, hopeless fight with himself. No, he changes the place where he stands. He crosses a threshold.

He enters "God's sanctuary." What is that? Does he mean the building in which the worshiping community meets? Does he enter the house of God's Word of Wisdom, which Jesus Sirach talks about later?

> He who peers through Wisdom's windows
>   will also listen at her doors;
> he who encamps near her house
>   will also fasten his tent peg to her walls;
> . . . .
> he will be sheltered by her from the heat
>   and will dwell in the midst of her glory.
>   (Sir. 14:23–24, 27)

At all events it is the place and the time where only one voice is heard, the voice which makes fifteen thousand other voices unimportant: "Be still, and know that I am God." It is the place where the prophets and, even more, the apostles point to the Word of God which has entered our history. It is the place where the unrest and ferment about other people find an end, and the endless treadmill of our own ego comes to a stop, and God himself, in his liberty, begins to speak and gives us new vision and educates us anew.

We talk about vacations for further education. Georges Bernanos wrote: "Five minutes of paradise will put everything right." How much education does a person need? Is anything really more important than a short time every day, and a little more time on Sundays, to listen to that "educative," re-forming, and re-creating voice, which acts on us through the messengers of the Bible? Our psalmist's crisis, at all events, did not end until he entered God's sanctuary. And now there is an immediate change. The circumstances that had upset him so much before no longer enrage him. Before, he had been full of envy when he saw these people getting more and more power undisturbed. Now he sees them soberly and objectively. He learns how to distinguish between what is only for a time and what is ultimate. He sees other facts too. Without God, everything that glitters is not gold. He sees that people who seemed so unassailable that for him they were a stumbling block are really standing on quicksands. Overnight, one of them disappears from the scene altogether, losing all his mighty influence at a single stroke.

But it is himself, above all, whom the psalmist sees with different eyes. When he was bitter and full of hurt feelings he was really a stupid ass, without understanding. Can't you hear him slap his forehead and exclaim: "I stood in front of you like an ox!" He had talked about difficult circumstances; but really it was only he himself who was being difficult. He thought and thought, and went round in circles until, in the quietness and light of the sanctuary, he came to his senses. Georg Neumark puts it in this way:

> Nor think amid the fiery trial
> That God hath cast thee off unheard,
> That he whose hopes meet no denial
> Must surely be of God preferred.
> Time passes and much change doth bring
> And sets a bound to everything.
> ("If Thou But Suffer God
> to Guide Thee.")

But it is not only other people and himself that he has learnt to judge more objectively. The most important thing in his new education is still to come. Now he can talk about God for the first time. How does he do this? Let us look at vv. 23–26.

> Nevertheless I was and am continually with thee;
>   thou dost hold my right hand.
> Thou dost guide me with thy counsel,
>   at the end—O glory!—thou wilt receive me.
> Whom do I need in heaven?
>   and if I am with thee I do not desire the earth.
> My flesh and my spirit may waste away,
>   but thou, God, are the strength of my life for ever.

The very structure of the language itself has become quite different. He is no longer talking *about* God; he is talking *with* God. Now that God has spoken to him, he can talk to God. "Thou dost guide me with thy counsel." Prayer is the true and primal way in which human beings talk about God. It is response to his encouragement and exhortation. In prayer we men and women can gratefully take him at his word. This Sunday has the name "Rogate"—"ask!" That means: you can pray! In our psalm God has now become the subject. He is the Thou to which every statement is related. Earlier (up to v. 22) the psalmist has talked basically about himself, though between whiles he also complained at length about the godless. Now his subject is God and nothing else. Unheard of in our world! But God becomes the subject.

"Nevertheless I was and am continually with thee." It sounds almost mystically exalted—if it had not been introduced by the extremely astringent confession: "Like a stupid ox I stood before you"—but all the same—even then—even in his stupidity—"before you." Even in his doubt, even in his bitterness, even in the hours when everything looked as if he was going to stumble and fall, when he himself dared not stretch out his hand to seize God's—even then: "you held my right hand." That is what he discovers about the past and the present. And this is the way he goes into the future: "Thou dost guide me with thy counsel." It began with his entry into the sanctuary, and what is ahead and what is to be done will emerge step by step. Every minute is given me by you, every opportunity.

The psalm persuades us to embody our trust in God in the form of direct address: you lead me with your counsel, your care for my spirit accompanies me; in the meditation on your Word in moments of quiet, in something said by a messenger whom you have sent me, in the church I attend. God's guidance is more important than anything else in the world. The psalmist has been led out of his inner disintegration step by step, not through an overall program. What has saved him are the "five minutes of paradise," not a general survey of God and the problems of the world. And yet he can still extend his certainty explicitly to some "boundary" problems. What is going to happen at the end? What about a final "afterward"? "You will receive me!" Nothing could be briefer, nothing could be more full of trust. This is not a detailed conception about being "carried off to heaven," of the kind the narrator presented when he told how the prophet Elijah was "taken up into heaven," or of the kind indicated, at least, in Psalm 49. Nor does the psalmist develop any idea of resurrection. Only this one Hebrew word, *lakachta*, "you take me." It is a word which is also used in the Old Testament when a man "takes" his wife to him in the most intimate sense. So what the sentence expresses is pure, astonished gratitude to God: "At the end—O glory—you will take me!"

Then the writer thinks of the possibility of final loneliness. Ideas about heaven or mythical powers no longer have any force. Earth with its treasures and with its human beings withdraws too. And yet nothing will be lacking, since he can say "I shall be with you." "With you"—the words are repeated three times (vv. 22, 23, 35). It can hardly be translated into explanatory language. It is distilled experience and has to find its exposition in life.

A student told us that he sometimes tried to imagine living in a world in which God for him didn't exist. He would rather undergo a severe illness, with God. He would rather give up his studies, with God—anything rather than to have to go on living in a world without God. This is the way someone today expresses the experience of God's presence. "If only I am beside you, everything in heaven and earth is of purely secondary importance."

Or a woman student says: If I can only once seize on the discovery that in spite of everything, for me God is good, then I can be free of all the obsessions under which our generation suffers so horribly—the conviction that, mind and body, we are hopelessly at the mercy of inexorable laws; then I can say: and if I have to go through hell, then I will go through hell—with you.

"I am with you." What a divine abundance is perceived here! What closeness. What all-sufficiency. The psalmist has anticipated the words in Bach's motet: "Hence!—Hence!—Hence! all fears and sadness, for the Lord of gladness, Jesus enters in."

Finally he faces up to the possibility that body and mind will decay. Perhaps this was the situation he was already in when he was writing, since he talks earlier about his daily torments, comparing them with the rude health of the godless. There is not a syllable here about rehabilitation. How close this man brings us to the crucified Jesus in everything he says! "If we have died with him we shall also live with him." He talks quite clearly about the decay of the body and the mind; but he equally clearly calls God the support of his life, his bread for ever. No "But how?" bothers him. Everything is hidden in his God. The important thing is God's peace, not prosperity. All fantasy is kept in bounds by faith. But for the future the endangered human being is hidden in the fullness of God, just as he was earlier held by God's hand even in his asinine stupidity. So the autobiography of a doubter ends in over-whelming assurance—or, to be more precise, in the assurance of a man who has been overwhelmed. When the psalmist entered the sanctuary he was conquered by the consolations of the One who was present. By telling us about the long road he has traveled, he has shown how right his main theme at the beginning is: "In spite of everything, God is good to the upright, to those who are pure in heart." He does not finish with-out developing the certainty of his experience through a contrast. Let us look at vv. 27–28:

> For lo, those who are far from thee will be lost;
>   thou bringest to silence all those who are false to thee.
> But for me it is good to come closer to God.
>   I have placed my trust in the Lord.
>   Therefore I tell of all thy works.

The alternative confronts us with a decision. It is not two different intel-lectual standpoints which are being offered for us to choose from, but two different directions in which men and women can move. The one draws away from God. In practical terms this means drawing away from the sanctuaries of the Word that dwells among us. Modern people pro-test at the idea that this means that they will lose themselves: "Thou bringest to silence all those who are false to thee." But the psalmist would find it inhumane, even intolerant, to hold his tongue about this danger. A good many people will feel bound to confirm this experience. If my steps move away from the way of God, it brings me into terrible entanglements. We do ourselves immense damage every day if we do not allow ourselves to be guided by the knowledge of this experience. We should notice that the psalmist doesn't pontificate about this experi-ence as if it were a truth straight from heaven (as the godless do, when they talk down to other people). He utters it prayerfully before God, as if he were warning himself first of all about new dangers.

He has discovered that the Good is to be found in the opposite direction: to move closer to God. So the psalmist gives us an important answer to the third question which the opening sentences provoked: who can reckon with God's goodness? Who is so sincere that the promise can apply to him? His experience does not allow him to exclude the possibility that a person may be on the verge of slipping—indeed that he did actually fall, in his bitterness and foolishness. But he didn't remain prostrate. He crossed the threshold into the room in which the Word of God became flesh. For us it is clearer still that God is not a vague dream, but that he took on historical dimensions in Jesus Christ. God has surrendered himself to us in all his love so that we may put all our trust in him. "This is my joy, that I hold fast to God," was Luther's version of this last verse of our psalm. To come near to God—that is good. This is the only thing that is good. The direction, the trend, is the important thing. "I put my trust in the Lord." This trust is the source of everything else. In the light of this trust a whole life becomes clear. "So I will tell of all your works." He doesn't keep them to himself. He tells what he has experienced, so that he can help other people not to stick fast in their difficulties; so that he can help us not to stick fast in ours. Amen.

The peace of God which passes all understanding keep our hearts and minds in Christ Jesus. Amen.

6

The Dawn of Peace

Sermon on Isaiah 9:2–7*

The people that walks in darkness
   sees a great light,
and over those who dwell in a land of deep darkness
   on them a light shines.
Thou awakest loud jubilation,
   thou makest great the joy.
They rejoice before thee
   as with joy at the harvest,
   as men rejoice when they divide the spoil.
For the yoke of their burden,
   and the staff for their shoulder,
   and the rod of their oppressor,
   thou hast broken as on the day of Midian.
For every boot of the tramping warrior in battle tumult
   and every garment rolled in blood
   will be burnt as fuel for the fire.
For to us a child is born,
   to us a son is given;
and the government rests on his shoulder;
   and he is called "Wonderful Counselor, God-Hero,
   Everlasting Father, Prince of Peace;"
so that his kingdom will be great and of peace
   there will be no end
upon the throne of David and in his kingdom,
   so that he may strengthen and uphold it
through justice and righteousness
   from this time forth and for evermore.
The zeal of the Lord of Hosts will do this.

---

*Preached in the university service in Mainz on the Second Sunday after Epiphany, 1962.

It is wonderful that this Word could be spoken to us human beings at all. We can learn from this prophetic Word what Jesus means for us today and tomorrow. And that means: we can learn what the decisive thing for us really is, today and tomorrow.

A vision was confided to the prophet here. He was permitted to see the dawn of a completely new day for the world, a universal kingdom of peace without end. But what was his actual, real life experience? First of all he could only see the Assyrian Empire—the great military power of his day—growing stronger and stronger. It is true that in his old age he also saw the troops of Assyria coming to a halt before the gates of Jerusalem and having to withdraw without achieving their objective; and his great-grandchildren saw Assyria's empire in a state of complete decline. But Assyria was replaced by another empire, and neither the prophet nor his listeners and readers ever saw installed in Jerusalem a ruler belonging to David's dynasty the foundation of whose throne was peace without end, a ruler who was not again replaced by any other. Isaiah himself has something to say about these disappointments: "But I will wait for the Lord, who is now hiding his face" (8:17). He was sure that in "the zeal of the Lord of Hosts" (9:7), liberty and the faithfulness of God could never be in opposition to one another (28:23–29). So when God entrusted him with this anticipation of the future, he passed it on to his disciples in writing "as a witness for a future day" (30:8). In some marvelous way it was so provided that this expectation—unlike other images of hope—continued to be proclaimed as a living message from generation to generation. Two hundred years later, after the tremendous catastrophe of the Babylonian exile, we have evidence that the same word kindled a fire once more. An unknown voice (Isaiah 60) takes up the message of the great light (9:2) and reawakens Jerusalem's hope, in spite of her despondency: "Arise, shine; for your light is coming!" (60:1), "Nations shall come to this light!" (v. 3). So faith remains on the move in the direction of the future, nourished by the knowledge that even in the darkness of judgment what was being fulfilled was simply the Word of God that had already been proclaimed.

Faith remains on the move in the direction of the future until, round Jesus of Nazareth, the voices of faith swell as never before, proclaiming in breathless adoration or with missionary power: "He is the light of the world!" "He is our peace!" "He is the lord of all the other lords!" But reason strives to be honest and asks: "Is he really the one who was to come?" He, who was so poor, who is so controversial, who came to grief so quickly? But faith wants to be no less honest and, ever since Easter, throughout the centuries, in spite of everything the worldly wise find conceivable, has to acknowledge: "He, just he, is the very one!" With his goodly word a final decision has been made among us. We have seen death shrink back before his love. With him a blessing radiates out from Israel to the gentile nations of the world, and many, many people have been brought to a truly new life. You and I who are here this morning belong to this long procession. We are links in this chain of the hopeful and the waiting, the disappointed and the disheartened, the men and women who have been blessed and enlightened, and the ones who have questioned and doubted. In this unbroken line we listen to the voice which set the trek on the move and leads it toward its goal. Without this prophetic voice we are in danger of expecting too little of Jesus, whose entry into our human world we have just celebrated—of expecting too little, today and tomorrow. Without that voice we cannot really understand properly what our situation is on the way along which we are being led. How, then, does our faith in Jesus acquire support, orientation, and sustenance through the prophetic word of the Old Testament? What this word does is to help us to recognize the dimensions of the gift God has given us in Jesus.

With Jesus the morning of a wholly new world has broken.

> The people that walks in darkness,
>   sees a great light,
> and over those who dwell in a land of deep darkness
>   on them a light shines.

The prophet has in his mind's eye people who are suffering under the fearful military domination of the Assyrian empire in all its brutality, people who are enduring unspeakable terrors and agonies. Men and women who once experienced God's covenant and help see themselves thrown into deep darkness, into the land of the dead, the land from which there is no return (Job 10:21–22) and in which there is no hope. What we are looking at here is the picture of our profound perplexity and helplessness about the East–West conflict. Christianity—even if it makes its voice heard in New Delhi—is not capable of proving itself a wonderful counselor, the father of a new future, the prince of peace. On the contrary, it is dragged into the vortex of dissension. Christians are not the light. They are the people who walk in darkness. They are ourselves.

And yet the great light has come into view. It is more than a prophetic vision. With Jesus the morning sun has risen over the somber terrain. We mistake him if we compare him with the lanterns and headlights we use to help us find our way in the night. With him dawn breaks on the morning of a new divine creation of God's among us. A new world is beginning. This and nothing less than this is the whole dimension of the gift of God in the appearance of Jesus. For this we dwellers in the land of shadows should rub our sleepy eyes. The morning of a new humanity has already dawned on the people in darkness. Not with us. But for us and for all.

Before the prophet shows exactly what he means, he talks about the effect of this dawn—the jubilation and the great joy. Laughter and singing had been frozen into silence, but now people thaw out in the warmth of the new light. It is like the happiness of an abundant harvest, or as if an evil war has come to a good end. A new era has dawned, new time for the good life.

The prophet cannot talk about the joy of it all without praise and adoration of the One who has made it possible:

> *Thou* awakest loud jubilation,
> *thou* makest great the joy.
> They rejoice before *thee*. . . .

For this is the joy of people who are unable to rejoice of their own accord any more. This is joy over God's new creative act. Whatever really cheers us and wakes true joy is a happening between God and us, and takes place in his presence.

So what is really happening? What is the reason for the outbreak of jubilation? Why is joy going to be the keynote of the new world that is dawning? The prophet tells us the reason in the terms of his own time:

> The yoke of their burden,
> and the stick for their shoulder
> and the rod of their taskmaster
> thou hast broken as on the day of Midian.

Isaiah is thinking of the Assyrian oppressors. God can equip empires with weapons in order to punish and teach his people. But he can also strike these weapons out of their hands, and he will do so, just as he did once in the days of Gideon, with the predatory Midianites. People who think that in our world the whole of life is dependent on the decisions of the great powers ought to know that this is not true, either in personal life or generally. This became much clearer when the new world dawned in Jesus than it was in the prophetic pre-view. Anyone who encounters the authoritative promise of Jesus—in the Beatitudes for example; anyone who hears the crucified Jesus proclaimed as the one who is risen and alive; anyone who learns that his cross is only one more reason— indeed the ultimate reason—for recognizing him as the daybreak of the new world: that person will know with absolute certainty that the last word does not lie with the great powers. And even in their less-than-final decisions only the Father of Jesus is at work. These powers can only be viewed as secondary, temporary instruments; they can only enjoy the status of a passing world. With Jesus the fear of these powers and anxiety about their decisions is replaced by a tremendous joy over the absolute sovereignty of God: "God's word, for all their craft and force, one moment shall not linger." That should be the keynote of our expectations for the coming year, for we are all called to be citizens of this new world.

The second reason for rejoicing which the prophet gives is this:

> Every army boot that tramps by
> and every coat that is rolled in blood
> is to be thrown into the fire
> as food for the flames!

Isaiah is thinking of the military cloaks of the Assyrians and their army boots. Luther gave a general interpretation of what the prophet meant when he said: "All the arms of those who arm with vehemence shall be burnt." Israel is not to use these arms for her own purposes, for example. They are intended for one end only: they are to be destroyed. Isaiah says exactly the same thing elsewhere, too, when he sees the light of a new world flood out from Israel to all nations:

59

> They shall beat their swords into ploughshares,
> and their spears into pruning hooks.
>
> (Isa. 2:4)

And then Jesus gives us the clear commandment: "Love your enemies. Bless those that curse you. Do good to those who hate you. Pray for those who insult you and persecute you, so that you may be the children of your Father who is in heaven." Humanity, and even Christians, are moving only very hesitantly out of their darkness and into the light of this unequivocal Word. And yet we are nonetheless advancing toward the day when all weapons will have to fall silent. Yes, even in this period of gigantic military threats and armaments, the resurrection of the crucified Jesus means that these threats and these armaments cannot contribute anything to the life of a new world. All they can do is to push the old world further toward its final end. The world which is arming for war is a world that belongs to the past. Ever since Isaiah, and ever since Jesus, joy in the new world of God means joy over the annihilation of all the materials of war.

We must think about this very carefully, for the Christian church is shockingly in arrears with its insights in this respect. That is why it is only in so feeble a degree the light of the world, and that is why it partakes so much of the world's darkness: because it hides the light that has dawned in Jesus under the bushel of the old world's laws. The young churches can help us here. A native chief from one of the South Sea Islands says this in an address to his people: "The first thing that God did was that through the papalagi (the white missionaries) he took away all our firearms and all our other weapons from us, so that we could live together like good Christians; for you know the words of God, telling us that we should all love one another and should not kill, which is his highest commandment. We gave up our weapons and since then no wars have devastated our islands, and each one respects the other as his brother. . . . The papalagi brought us the light which lit a fire in our hearts and filled our senses with happiness and gratitude. He had that light earlier than we. The papalagi already stood in the light when the eldest among us were not yet born. But he only holds the light in his outstretched hand, to give light to others. He himself, his own body, stands in the darkness, and his heart is far from God. Nothing is more difficult for me, nothing fills my heart with greater sadness, dear children of the many islands, than to have to tell you this. But we must not and will not deceive ourselves about the papalagi, so that he does not draw us into his own darkness. He brought us God's word. He understood it with his lips and with his head, but not with his body. The light has not invaded him in such a way that he can reflect it, and that wherever it shines, everything shines in the light that streams from his heart."

Which of us may ignore what is being said here? We are beginning to draw the proper conclusions, though far too hesitantly. One of them would seem to be that in the German Federal Republic preachers of the Gospel are exempted from military service. But what kind of interpretation of the Gospel is this? Don't all the people who live from the Gospel of the new world belong in the light of the new day in exactly the same way? But here too one way is open to us: we have the right to become conscientious objectors. We have that right. Are we really aware of the inward struggle our fellow students in Eastern Europe have to go through about this? Do we realize that they perhaps have to pay with their lives for what is one of our legal rights? Are we sufficiently conscious of the fact that for people over there it is a serious—even a disabling—political matter when, here in the West, Christians in their masses believe that they do not have to draw the same conclusion as those Christians in the South Seas? And are we aware, on the other hand, what a helpful political act it would be for our brothers and sisters in the East if we did so? At least insights about this matter are maturing sufficiently for them to be ripe for inclusion in the catechism. The new German Protestant catechism is an encouraging sign. After almost nine years of work the Synod of the Evangelical Church in the Rhineland released it last week to be tried out in local coigregations. H re the explan tion of the commandment "You shall not kill" goes on, in its second paragraph: "God does not want the nations to wage war against one another. We should therefore resist jingoism and militarism and should strive with all our powers for peace in the world." All weapons belong in the fire: our prophetic Word tells us that this is part of the joy over the new day of God.

I do not want to preach peace and sow dissension here. I know that some people have serious doubts about conscientious objection. But I am more concerned still in case we are only entering theoretically—in thought, but not wholly, which means not with complete joy—into the light of the new day which the prophet announced and which dawned in Jesus. For this joy can and should be nourished every single day, if we carry all our quarrels and all our many and manifold disputes with us into the dawn of the new creation.

At this point, the third reason Isaiah gives for his prophecy provides us with a further ground for great joy. Using the concepts of his time, the prophet sees the birth of a child who will ascend the throne of David and from there will take over the rule of the whole world in a kingdom of complete peace without end. In other sayings, Isaiah depicted the new era as something quite different; and other prophets painted it differently again. But they were all one in their conviction that, after his judgments had fallen on his people of old, God would bring about in Israel the beginning of something entirely new for the whole world; and that what was intended here was a true rebirth of the real, material world. And yet they never saw the liberty of God's zeal as in any way contrasting with his faithfulness to his Word. It is in accordance with this that the New Testament writings, in spite of all their differences, are at one in saying that the Jesus who was born so late and who was so unkingly is the ruler of the world; that the One who was so disputed is peace in person; that the Jesus whom they so swiftly crucified is the One whose kingdom shall have no end.

This means that in the person of Jesus the new universal day has really dawned for men and women. Here, in the twentieth century, our faith can be encouraged by what the prophet has to say. How he rejoices in his preview of the future!

> A child has been born for us,
>   a son has been given us,
>   and the government will be on his shoulders.

What he says is probably meant only for the small circle of his disciples: "born for us! given to us!" But he is certain at the same time that this child—born only as yet in a vision—will be entrusted with universal rule. In much the same way we may see the actual, veritable ruler of the world in the Word made flesh, which is what the despised Jesus is. It is only then that we shall resolutely live from his Word every day. Then we shall rightly apply to Jesus those names of the Messiah which Isaiah lists. Here the prophet was deliberately picking up titles applied to the pharaohs, who in his time counted as the models of true universal rule. The whole emphasis lies on the final name "Prince of Peace." This was led up to in v. 5, where all armaments are thrown into the fire, and is developed in v. 7:

> The bounds of his kingdom will be wide
> and of peace there will be no end.

Elsewhere the extension of rule always means war and the shedding of blood. With this prince the opposite is the case. Only the person who understands him wholly and completely as the ruler of peace can understand his universal rule. This cannot be clearer than it is in Jesus; for as the one who was crucified he renounces all force, practices unconditional forgiveness, and in this way conquers the world. But his disciples can only serve him by taking up their cross after him, and by resolutely putting their swords in their sheaths in the power and faithfulness of his love and forgiveness. If we desire honestly to respect his rule over the world as the only true one, then we will daily practice peacemaking, resolving differences between people, and bringing people together instead of driving them apart, in joy over the new world. We need far more peace in small things. For peace is the keynote of the new world that has dawned—the world that is coming, the world that is the ultimate world.

This is the last thing which Isaiah tells us: "His peace will have no end." "His sovereignty will last from this time forth and for evermore." Isaiah does not so much help us to understand the Jesus of nineteen hundred years ago—the evangelists can do that better. What he does is to lead us to understand Jesus better in our own day, and to see him in the context of the future. Anyone who comes to Jesus and wholeheartedly renounces everything that is warlike stands side by side with the Lord of the future, the "Father of the Future" (which is probably a better translation of the throne name "Everlasting Father"). We are standing beside the One in whom "God's heroic power" among us does new work. We are beside the One who "plans what is wonderful," advises, and implements, the One who with his love achieves with power what seems to us unattainable and impossible.

Let me sum up. In faith we are allowed to see the One who *has* come and the One who *will* come as one and the same; just as Isaiah looks simultaneously at the child and at the final universal ruler of peace. How little of the future Isaiah was able to survey! But, in absolute confidence in God's ardent zeal, he already lived in entire joy before him. How much more reason we have to do this! In Jesus the new day has dawned for us who are in darkness. To maintain this joy before him means daily taking his Word a good deal more seriously than the things this passing world imposes on us. It means heeding his complete will toward peace more than all our inclinations toward enmity. It means firmly putting dialogue with him before everything that lies ahead, so that we do not become victims of what is really past and done with. For the joy is this: that it is he and he alone who brings about the new world.

7

The Hope of the Disappointed

Sermon on Isaiah 63:15—64:3*

Look down from heaven and see,
    from thy holy and glorious habitation.
Where is now thy zeal and thy might?
    The yearning of thy heart and thy compassion?
For thou art our Father.
    For Abraham does not know us
        and Israel does not acknowledge us.
Thou, O Lord, art our Father.
    "Our Redeemer," that is of old thy name.
O Lord, why dost thou make us err from thy ways
    and harden our heart, so that we fear thee not?
Change this for the sake of thy servants,
    for the tribes that are thy heritage.
Why do the godless stride through thy temple?
Why do our adversaries tread down thy sanctuary?
We have become like those over whom thou hast never ruled,
    like people who have never been called by thy name.
O that thou wouldst rend the heavens and come down,
    that the mountains might melt at thy presence—
as when fire kindles brushwood
    and as fire causes water to boil—
to make thy name known to thy adversaries,
    and that the nations might tremble at thy presence,
when thou doest astonishing things which we look not for,
    and which no one saw of old.
No ear has heard, no eye has seen a God besides thee
    who does such good to those who wait for him.

---

*Preached in the university service in the Peterskirche, Heidelberg, on the first Sunday in Advent, November 28, 1971.

Lord, send forth your light and your truth that they may lead us. Amen.

I wonder which sentence in this tremendous and terrible prayer touched you most directly? What echoed the words of your own heart? Was it that seared admission "We have become like those over whom thou hast never ruled"? Or do you join in with the insistent questions: "Where is now thy zeal, where is thy might, where is thy compassion? Why dost thou make us err? Why dost thou harden our hearts?" Did you too cry out for the heavens to be rent apart and for God to become a real presence on earth? Or does one or the other of you perhaps already belong to the avant-garde who has to say in all honesty: "No ear has heard, no eye has seen a God besides thee who does such good to those who wait for him"?

"Who wait for him"—perhaps this is the point where, different as we are, we can join our voices most easily. "To wait steadfastly for him"— that is surely also the underlying theme running right through this prayer. Waiting for the unexpected could weld us all into a congregation that is gathered into the movement of this prayer of longing.

What else can we do but wait? We must make this clear to ourselves from this prayer. Isn't our whole life today characterized by God's absence? Where in our present-day lives do we see anything of what our forefathers told us about the intervening lightning of God's glance, the zeal of his intervention and his transcending power? Where do we see any sign that God's heart is stirred because our bewilderment and confusion drive him to compassion? Where? Where? Is it shocking to put a series of question marks after God's name? This is what our prayer does. Would it perhaps be more "religious" to accept the fact that God is leaving the world to itself? Should we hold our tongues about the generally accepted impression that nowadays, in the years we are living through, God no longer thinks our planet worth a glance? Our prayer puts its stormy questions just as the crucified God put his: "My God, why hast thou forsaken me?" We should ask just as persistently and plead just as perseveringly: "Now look down from heaven! Look down from your holy and glorious habitation! Look on us, even if your glance confounds us! Do not withdraw or turn a deaf ear to us!" What else can we do but wait for him?

Can we remain human beings at all if we do not suffer because God has closed himself against us? "For thou art after all our Father. For

Abraham does not know us and Israel does not acknowledge us." Why doesn't Abraham know us? Because he belongs to a past generation. Our human fathers and forefathers cannot help us. Tradition cannot save us. Unless, indeed, it had pointed us to the Father of the future and told us his name "from of old": "our Redeemer." It is him alone we have to thank for our own specific, individual lives. He alone can liberate us specifically for the future. What else can we do but wait for him? But what is he really doing here and now?

The answer takes the form of new, tormenting questions: "Lord, why dost thou make us err from thy ways and harden our heart, so that we fear thee not?" I wonder whether some of us, at least, can echo these terrible questions? Is it only a few of us who have felt our feet slipping? Which of us has not landed in the broad ditch which dazzled us, like a supermarket with its three neon-lit catchwords, security, success, sex? These slogans have laid us open to manipulation. Like the Galatians, we are confronted with Paul's question: "Are you so foolish? Having begun with the Spirit, are you now ending with the flesh?" (Gal. 3:3). When these people talk about the hardened hearts which do not fear God, they are not talking about some stranger or other. They are talking about themselves, in the dire need into which the eclipse of God has plunged them. These people have surely heard the reproach: "What right have you to recite my statutes, or to take my covenant on your lips? For you hate discipline and you cast my words behind you." Which of us knows the compulsion to throw away the word which speaks to us in the voice of conscience? Which of us knows it because he has prayed dozens of times to be freed from this compulsion? But in vain. This person, and this person alone, understands this terrible question: "Why, O Lord, dost thou make us err from thy ways? Why dost thou harden our heart, so that we fear thee not?" It isn't the wicked world around us; it isn't our own personal weakness; no, it is God himself who is indicted because of this compulsive doom.

What else can we do but wait for him? "Turn back, change this for the sake of thy servants, the tribes that are thy heritage." Our conversion is impossible. We have tried and failed. We are incapable. Only God himself could bring about the change.

Even our venerable institutions cannot do this any longer. The questions to God probe on: "Why do the wicked despise thy temple? Why do our adversaries tread down thy sanctuary?" Isn't the church too becoming the playground for conflicting interests? It is not easy to confute the ironical view that God is conspicuous by his absence, and in the Christian church most of all. What else can we do but wait for him? Where is Advent? Where can we look for his arrival?

For in despair the community of God's people has to confess that "we have become like those over whom thou hast never ruled, like people who have never been called by thy name." What a phrase! When the name "David" was proclaimed over Rabbat Ammon, for example, it meant that the city was declared to be David's property; it was under his protection and he looked after it. If the name of God is proclaimed over men and women, they are wholly subject to him, to his directives and his care. But we have become like people over whom his Name has never been proclaimed. Where does the Christian community show that it is any different from other human associations? Where does it show that it has been led by God into liberty, into joy and into peace? Where does it become evident to people that we are not without a ruler—that, in the happiest sense of the word, we are "under command"? And if we echo, "We have become like those over whom thou hast never ruled," does it sound sad, or does it really sound proud? Do we feel betrayed— or emancipated? Or are we perhaps both—emancipated *and* betrayed? Again: what else can we do but wait for him? Our ancient prayer sharpens our perceptions, so that we can see that we are suffering so deeply largely because God has withdrawn and closed himself against us. And it is only God himself who can bring about the new beginning.

That is why we are now led on to the cry "O that thou wouldst rend the heavens and come down!" It is only against the dark background of our real situation as it has been shown to us that we realize the urgency of this Advent prayer. It implores the one thing needful: the coming into our midst of the One who is absent. It protests against God's dwelling in an unreachable upper story, in the abstraction of some higher spirituality. It pleads to God to go out and in on the ground floor. It wants to see the heaven of two thousand years that divides us from Jesus torn into shreds, and implores him to come to us. Countless words about him pass over our heads and no longer make any impact. Now we call for the one Word in which he himself comes to us. Today. Christians are reminded of nothing less than this when, as the old year rolls on, they arrive at Advent. A thousand bewildering notions occur to the world and the Christian church too. But what hardly ever occurs to us is the thing that is essential and the thing that is really helpful. Here we ask for the occurrence of God's intervention so that something better may occur to us too. To expect this and to wait for it resolutely are what this first Advent Sunday calls us to do during the coming weeks. Advent expects the coming of the necessary, helpful, joyful intervention which liberates us. The old cry did not die away unheard. The heaven opened over Jesus of Nazareth, his disciples say, and they live their lives from that fact. It is because of this that the New Testament breathes his Spirit. Jesus is the intervening event, the arrival and the presence of God down here, on earth. People have gathered in his name down to the present day—down to this very moment, when we too are gathered together; and this is largely because, from that early time onward, the cry for the heaven to be torn apart has always been heard, from generation to generation, down to our own. That is why we too are permitted to hope again for his coming, in our time, in our year, in our fathomless difficulties and uncertainties.

Hope can grow in us simply because we join in this ancient prayer. And his coming can already take place in that very act of hope. With the very petition, the words already begin to sense the idea of the coming—in a trust nourished by experience. "No ear has heard, no eye has seen a God besides thee who does such good to those who wait for him." Talking about Jesus, Paul writes that it has come about "as it is written." How does the good thing for the people who wait for him come about, as God again rends the heavens apart and descends?

It comes about in such a way that "the mountains melt at his presence." When he enters, unsurmountable obstacles dissolve into nothingness. We can discover this for ourselves.

"As when fire kindles brushwood!" Can you hear it crackle? Can you see the flames licking up the heap of dry wood? Do you see it spread with raging speed and every twig turn into pure flame? John the Baptist tells us that this is what it is like when the Messiah baptizes his people with the Holy Spirit and with fire. When his flames overrun us, then the dead wood of the church and the dry thickets of our own lives turn into something full of light and warmth again—in just the degree to which the old life is burnt up.

"As fire causes water to boil." This is what it is like when God comes to us on the ground floor: cold water becomes warm. When we were children we watched it happen, and perhaps even now you enjoy seeing the first bubbles rise and the water beginning to simmer and to effervesce. The water boils, the kettle whistles, and an old steam engine gets under way. We can learn how "fire causes water to boil" with the coming of his Spirit. "To make thy name known to thy adversaries, and that the nations might tremble at thy presence." This is how Jesus wanted to light a fire upon earth, and waited for it soon to burn. Why, really, do the nations tremble before this fire? It was kindled together with the cross of his self-surrender. That is why God has given him the name that is above every name. What conclusion do we have to draw? The nations must completely change their ways of doing things. In political terms, this means that they must recognize the guilt of their warlike self-assertion and of every single warlike attitude. This is what Advent means today: the study of war will be replaced by research into peace—replaced, not merely supplemented. Armaments will give way to the implements for peace. Maneuvers for peace will take the place of military ones. The world is gradually realizing that it will be digging its own grave in all sectors of life if these things remain empty phrases. But Advent is needed, the intervention of Christ's fire, if the great revolution is to become a real event in the small things of life, in the church, and on the world stage.

"When thou doest astonishing things which we look not for, and which no one saw of old." Christ's advent is never a reversion to what is old—to what has always been. It is the entry of the unexpected. That is why it is the only hope for people who are disappointed in the whole course the world has taken hitherto. In the Christian church, men and women who have been disappointed in all sectors of life can come together. Here, disappointed as they are, they can learn to hope, even for what has, up to now, never been at all. Economically, Advent means that the greatest happiness is to be found not in continually growing prosperity but in better sharing—in our world economy, in our national economy, in our businesses, in our domestic affairs. In the social context, Advent means recognizing his coming—more: his presence—in the hungry, in strangers, in the sick, and in people who are in prison.

This means that Advent is probably much nearer than we think. Luther could admonish his readers: "Stop gaping up to heaven! Here you have it—here below!" He was thinking of the Lord's Supper, in which Jesus visits us hungry, alien, sick, and imprisoned men and women, and in which we prisoners-at-the-bar are acquitted. And he was thinking of the Word, the Word of Jesus' witnesses; that the Word may kindle its fire again—this is what we should be expectantly waiting for. "Stop gaping up to heaven! Here you have it—here below!" But he is also pointing to Jesus' coming in the least of his brethren. When we cry out in church: "O that thou wouldst rend the heavens and come down!" then we should be alive to the places where God is to be found, in the immediate radius of the church, and farther off, and perhaps soon at the church's very doors, so that we stumble over him, and can drive right past him in our cars: God in the hospitals, God in the prisons, God in the form of a drug addict, God in the figure of an immigrant worker, God in the member of the family we despise, in the "outsider," the colleague we turn up our noses at and ignore. Not passing these people by can mean not missing Advent either.

Advent requires us to be alert. It is hypocrisy if we cry to God without expecting something—something quite specific. None of us should expect to cry in vain: "O if you would only rend the heavens and take concrete form on earth!" Advent is the arrival of the unexpected thing which no one saw of old. I should like you to take this last sentence of this prayer more seriously than everything that precedes it, even if the previous sentences may initially have seemed to echo more closely what you yourselves feel. The last sentence proclaims the hope of the disappointed. It leads us into new territory: "No ear has heard, no eye has seen a God besides thee, who does such good to those who wait for him." Your ear will be the first ear, when he comes now, again, in the Feast, in the Word, in the least of the brethren. Your eye will be the first eye, when he comes to us now, distraught as we are. Anyone who lives with this belongs to the avant-garde. In every coming to every individual person what happens is something unheard of. The fire wants to crackle through our parched brushwood. The blessing of Advent can begin even with the letter from a friend, or with the unexpected bottle of wine standing in front of my door. Complete fulfillment is promised to steadfast waiting. This is something we can all discover. Amen.

And may the peace of God which passes all understanding keep our hearts and our minds in Christ Jesus. Amen.

8

The Church—A Hopeless Case

Sermon on Ezekiel 37:1–14*

The hand of the Lord came upon me, and the Lord brought me out in the Spirit and set me down in the midst of a valley; and it was full of bones. And he led me round among them; and behold, there were very many upon the valley; and lo, they were very dry. And he said to me, "Son of man, can these bones live?" And I answered, "O Lord God, thou knowest." Again he said to me, "Proclaim to these bones, and say to them, O dry bones, hear the word of the Lord. Thus says the Lord God to these bones: Behold, I will cause breath to enter you, and you shall live. And I will lay sinews upon you, and will cause flesh to come upon you, and cover you with skin, and put breath in you, and you shall live; and you shall know that I am the Lord." So I proclaimed as I was commanded; and as I proclaimed there was a rustling, and behold, a movement; and the bones came together, bone to its bone. And as I looked, there were sinews on them, and flesh had come upon them, and skin had covered them; but there was no breath in them. Then he said to me, "Call the Spirit of life: come from the four winds, and breathe upon these slain, that they may live." And I proclaimed as he commanded me, and the breath of life came into them, and they lived and stood upon their feet, an exceedingly great host. Then he said to me, "Son of man, these bones are the whole house of Israel. Behold, they say, 'Our bones are dried up, and our hope is lost; we are clean cut off.' Therefore proclaim and say to them, Thus says the Lord God: Behold, I will open your graves, and raise you from your graves, O my people; and I will bring you home into the land of Israel. And you shall know that I am the Lord, when I open your graves, and raise you from your graves, O my people. And I will put my Spirit of life within you, and you shall live, and I will place you in your own land; then you shall know that I am the Lord. I have spoken and I will also do it, says the Lord."

---

*Preached in the university service in the Peterskirche, Heidelberg, on the Sunday Misericordias Domini, April 28, 1974, the beginning of the summer term.

Lord, do your work in us anew today, and say to our hearts, "Let there be light," so that all darkness may depart from us. Amen.

Imagine that you are in the situation this chapter describes. Eleven years earlier, the prophet had been carried off to Babylon with the high, the mighty from Jerusalem. They had hoped against hope for a speedy return home. But the prophet had proclaimed Jerusalem's downfall as the definite will of God. And now the messenger had just arrived with the news: the city has fallen! Even the temple has been burnt to the ground! New groups of people were deported. After 587 B.C. Israel had no country any longer, no city, no temple, and now, surely, no God either: no future. So little groups of despairing people gathered round Ezekiel, shrouded in the deepest depression (v. 11): "Our bones are dried up, and our hope is lost; we are clean cut off"—we are finished. Don't you feel that we fit quite well into this group around Ezekiel, if we think of ourselves as a Christian congregation? Hasn't the second Enlightenment posted up the Christian church's obituary notice even more conspicuously than the first? Isn't the post-Christian shrug of the shoulders we meet in many quarters today far worse than the anti-Christian attitudes of past decades? Haven't we often sat, lost, in a church that is much too large? And even if the pews have filled up somewhat, do we do anything but sit next to one another like mummies, each for himself, without any communication? "Our bones are dried up." Some of you may only have come here this morning with a good deal of skepticism. "Our hope is lost!" When I was in Berlin recently, I was told by someone who should know: the clergy here have most of their time taken up with funerals. Symptomatic! A lot of past and very little future. Death is assiduously making his rounds among us. We are cut off like dried-up flowers. "We are finished." Let me ask you a plain, unvarnished question: what do we, in all the various faculties, still expect from the university service on Sundays? There is no doubt that the results of an opinion poll would be devastating. We ourselves may not talk like those Israelites who had been deported to Babylon, but other people are saying just that ten times over.

The prophet has this complete resignation ringing in his ears; and he is not offered any soothing syrup of an analysis in reply. The prophet has the desolate viewpoint of his people radically confirmed. He begins with the account of a completely unusual, dramatic happening. He is given a vision. The dramatic event happens to him as he is "translated," "snatched up to heaven" (vv. 1, 2). "The hand of the Lord came upon me." He sees himself taken away into the vastness of the Babylonian plain. Once there, he discovers that it is full of human bones. Horrible! He even has to walk across the huge plain (v. 2) and convince himself that there is nothing here but bleached bones, scattered abroad, "very many" and "very dry." Every glance confirms that this is the finish. This is what the exiled community really looks like. It is just vegetating. Death's triumph is complete.

At the end of the gruesome walk, the voice of Ezekiel's God confronts him: "Son of man, can these bones live?" Isn't Babylon the final grave of Israel's historical existence? Isn't this the final implementation of the divine judgment that had been proclaimed?

Do we not have to see ourselves challenged in a similar way? Aren't the graves of Christian traditions being dug everywhere? No—there are not even graves. Things are as they are in the vision: the scattered limbs are allowed to lie round, to putrefy, and to dry up. Don't we have to expect the end of the twentieth century to be the end of the Christian churches? Is this not just what we deserve, since we have so largely departed from the path of discipleship? (Compare Ezek. 33:10: "Our transgressions and our sins are upon us, and we waste away because of them; how then can we live?")

The prophet answers the question that is put to him: "O Lord God, thou knowest." In the face of these dried-up bones he simply cannot imagine that there could ever be any new life in them. But he cannot, either, force God into the straitjacket of his own viewpoint. A tiny, thread-like flame of hope flickers up in his answer: "O Lord God, thou knowest."

Do we talk like this too, perhaps with an even stronger infusion of skepticism? But must we not first of all honestly bring what we know into our answer—our knowledge of the history that lies between 587 B.C. and A.D. 1974? We must not suppress this knowledge. For we know that even for ancient Israel Babylon did not remain the final grave, but that, through all its terrible catastrophes, down to our own day, Israel has continued to live through and suffer through its astonishing history. In spite of everything, doesn't the cross of Jesus tower unmistakably out of this history? Do we not have the testimony of Christ's tomb that this has become the final tomb of all Israel's guilt and the guilt of the whole of humanity? Hasn't Easter just reminded us of the voice of Christ which the early churches heard: "I live and you shall live also?" Isn't the whole history of the church quite evidently a tremendous history of the death and resurrection of the churches in the different parts of the world? Fifty Indonesian Christians are now studying in Heidelberg, most of them coming from young churches which are very much alive. What they see among us is a valley full of dry bones; and they are perhaps much more dismayed at the sight than we ourselves.

"Do you think that these bones can live again?" "O Lord God, thou knowest." We must surely say no less than Ezekiel, especially since among us a great deal of old, putrefied flesh still has to rot away.

But now everything depends on our allowing ourselves to be led on-ward, firmly and decisively, by Ezekiel's vision. Recognition of the fun-damentally desolate situation was only the beginning. Now the voice of God introduces two revolutionary acts.

The first command to Ezekiel is this (vv. 4–5): "Proclaim to these bones, and say to them, Hear the word of the Lord. I will cause the breath of life to enter into you that you may live again." So the begin-ning is when an individual hears the charge his God gives him. He does not have to hold a particular office. Ezekiel is not even addressed as prophet. He is generally called "Son of man"—that is, human being (vv. 3, 11).

What is he told to do? "Proclaim to these bones!" He is not, for exam-ple, asked to seek out particular, individual figures in whom there may perhaps still be a spark of life. No, humanly speaking no possibilities are expected to exist at all. Through his messenger God acts on people who are really incapable of listening.

What is the messenger to say to them? "Hear the word of the Lord. *I* will cause the breath of life to enter into you. . . . *I* will lay sinews upon you. . . . *I* will cause flesh to grow. . . . *I* will put breath in you. . . ." We know: today what is initially meant is the earthly community of God's people. This "I will," "I make," is what we are supposed to hear. We are no longer supposed to be bound by our own analyses or forecasts, or to be depressed by them. We are to hear the unequivocal declaration of the will of the living Lord. It is sealed in the saying of the risen Jesus. "I live, and you shall live also." Our ideologies and philosophies come and go. This promise will continually show itself to be true until the end of time.

"Living from the Spirit" is the overall theme for our services during this summer term, 1974. How does someone live from the Spirit? "So I proclaimed as I was commanded. And as I proclaimed there was a rustling, and behold, a movement" (v. 7). We must notice this proceeding very particularly. The instrument that God uses to raise the church and its members is the proclamation of his messenger. In the messenger's mouth the Word of God proves itself an efficacious word of power. It was through messengers that the church came into being after Easter; it was through messengers that the church was revived at the Reformation and in the congregations of the Confessing church; it was through messengers that the young churches came into being all over the world. So as a university congregation we have clearly to concentrate our expectations on the proclamation, and initially on the series of sermons to be heard during this term, Sunday for Sunday.

What happened at Ezekiel's proclamation? "As I proclaimed, there was a rustling, and behold, a movement; and the bones came together, bone to its bone." And sinews grow, and flesh, covered with skin.

Let me ask you, where do we hear a rustling and a movement in this academic congregation, with its scrupulous concern to be detached and critical? Perhaps a little when the collection plates are passed round? But how formally and stiffly we sit next to one another as a rule! Couldn't we show, by being a little livelier, that the Lord has brought us scattered bundles of bones together to a living body, in which one person is there to help and give delight to the other?

Let me tell you something that happened to me a few months ago. Last September I had a surprising and unforgettable experience. I was in St. Louis, Missouri, at Concordia Seminary, one of the largest Lutheran Seminaries in America. At the beginning of the autumn term, four hundred students and forty professors gathered for a service of worship. After we had joined in the confession, we were told: "There is now no condemnation for those who are in Christ Jesus. The peace of the Lord is with you. You are free." It was after this word of pardon that the unexpected thing happened. My neighbors right and left of me in the pew turned to one another and to me. Americans are not particularly lavish with handshaking, but now they shook hands, exchanged friendly glances, and affirmed to one another, "Peace be with you! The peace of the Lord! Peace!" People in front of us and behind turned round. One of the professors sped through the church to take his wife's hand; another hurried to a colleague who was having a particularly difficult time. Peace be with you! So the promise which we had all received passed from one person to the next. And the same thing happened week after week. *This* is what our passage is talking about. Here there was a rustling and a movement, bone to its bone. And then we went quietly, in renewed fellowship and friendship, to the Lord's Supper. You are thinking: American mentality! Was it nothing more than that? Isn't mutual stimulus something we are discovering in our ecumenical fellowship? Are there not quite a few American, Asian, African, sometimes Australian friends among us who leave our services shivering? Our fifty Indonesian brothers and sisters find it difficult to make contact with us. When I am taking up the collection I quite often see very sad, isolated people sitting at the back of the church. This week I have been thinking about the report that, in the last year or two, thirty-five young people have died through an overdose of drugs in Heidelberg; I have been wondering whether one of them may sometime have sat in this church and been left to himself here too?

Let me make a first suggestion. Couldn't we, at least, personally affirm to our neighbors to the right and left, and in front of us and behind, the blessing which we are all given at the end of the service? Couldn't we say, "God's blessing for the week!" or "Peace be with you!" or at least "Have a good Sunday!"—at least to a few people? Who knows what might come of it here and there? And then there are those pleasant few minutes standing round and talking after church, when we also meet the people we have just had an altercation with—a trivial one perhaps— perhaps less trivial. Don't we shake hands in a different way in the light of the blessing?

We should think about how we behave at the Lord's Supper too. There we hear regularly: "Accept one another as Christ has accepted us." Can we go on standing poker faced next to one another, as if we just had walk-on parts? And then pass one another by as we go to our homes? Should we not at least silently greet one or the other of the people who have stood beside us, even if they are strangers? Who knows what may come of it?

78

If the result of the preaching in this summer term is a rustle and a movement, then we shall grow much closer together as a university congregation. Our congregation here should be the source of new communication between the torn and estranged groups in our university. The purpose of this service this morning is no less than this: to bring new, fruitful life from the spirit of the biblical witnesses and from the spirit of Jesus. What did Ezekiel tell us? "As I proclaimed, the bones came together, bone to its bone."

But the movement of our stiff bones is only the beginning (v. 8): "As I looked, there were sinews on them" (if only some of us could act as sinews joining the scattered bones!) "and flesh had come upon them, and skin had covered them; but there was no breath of life in them." Ezekiel then tells of a second command: "Then he said to me, 'Call the Spirit of life: come from the four winds and breathe upon these slain, that they may live.'" Strange: the Spirit of life is to come "from the four winds"—what is meant are the four quarters of the earth. We must not think too narrowly about the Spirit of God. He is the Spirit from whom the whole creation has its life, the life which our scientists and doctors are concerned about, the life which our historians and philologists try to trace in all periods and all languages. Next Sunday we shall hear a sermon on Ps. 104:29-30, and then we shall hear more about that universal breath with which the Creator gives life to the whole created world. It is nothing other than this breath of the Creator that is meant for the whole world which is now to come upon that field of the dead in the church, as the life-giving wind of the Spirit.

Ezekiel goes on: "So I proclaimed as he commanded me. Then the breath of life came into them" (v. 10). We are permitted to expect just this for this congregation too. Don't be surprised! Those of us who are preaching this term also come from the four winds—from the most varied, indeed the most opposite directions, in our theological and political traditions and in our personal dispositions. But every one of us is charged to stir up among us that life from the Spirit which has begun with the Gospel of Jesus Christ and the history which the Bible proclaims for the whole world.

You can help. At the beginning you were all given a sheet of yellow paper. Think about, and write down, all the things that must not be forgotten in the thanksgiving and the intercession later, for our whole university, and for all our services during the coming term, so that the Creator Spirit may reach and renew many people even before Whitsun, as well as afterward. This is what we all need.

Our passage tells us about the people who have begun to live again (v. 10): ". . . and they stood upon their feet, an exceedingly great host." It is only when the Spirit of life comes that the bodies begin to move. The bottom half of your yellow sheets of paper is also meant for anyone who is going home from this service disappointed, because it hasn't given him or her what he or she needs. Here these people can ask to be visited, and other people can offer themselves as visitors. Perhaps the first visitors will only hear what the trouble is, and they can then get in touch with the competent person through the helpers' group. You will see that Ezekiel already put some people on their feet even when this service was being prepared. But we are promised that the workings of the Spirit will result in "an exceedingly great host." Not only the preacher, the chapter, the helpers' group, hostesses, and stewards want to set the wind of the Spirit in motion; many other people in the congregation want to do the same.

You will have time immediately after the sermon to fill up these sheets of paper, if you would like to. A rustling is expected! Kind people will be ready with ballpoint pens, and will collect the papers for the final prayer. Where visits are concerned, you can also give up your papers on your way out. God's life-giving Spirit does not merely give people ideas. He also moves hands and feet, so that we can gladly turn to one another.

At the end the prophet merely tells how he was commissioned to tell his despondent people briefly and concisely what his vision amounted to. Here our attention is caught by a sentence which already occurred at the end of v. 6, and which is again repeated twice in vv. 13–14; and for us too this sentence is the real purpose of the whole message: "You shall know that I am the Lord."

It is with the expectation of knowing this that we can gather together now. This is what we expect for today, for this week, for this term, and for our whole lives. At the end we shall discover that we ourselves are not the masters of the life for which God rouses us and which he brings into movement among us through his Word; nor are we delivered over to other masters either, whether they are nameless or renowned. And it is good that this is so. Verse 14 explains: I will put "my Spirit" *within you*. The Spirit of God and of Jesus Christ will give every one of us the new ability to live from day to day, alert to the presence of the Spirit, not frittering away our energies, not undertaking too much, not wandering along half awake—and half awakened—but taking the straight path instead of the crooked one. Every Sunday should help take us a little further—and the Bible too, as our daily bread. "The words that I have spoken to you," says Jesus, "are spirit and life." In the Bible and in worship we can quite specifically experience the Spirit of the Lord, who has set out on the way to us as our friendly companion.

For, as our final experience, we can also be sure about what Ezekiel is told last of all: "I have spoken, and I will also do it." The sentence is intended to drive away our mistrust. We complicated people need just this simple promise. It will prove itself through all contradictions and all disappointments, as surely as the crucified and buried Jesus is the risen Lord.

I should like you all to take this assurance with you into the term ahead, with the concentrated expectation that you too will discover by experience that Jesus Christ creates new life. You can then establish peace, repose, and kindness in the midst of all the difficulties there may be in the university and in this city. It was in this assurance that they sang in St. Louis:

> Celebrate your bold election!
> You are born for resurrection.

Amen.

9

For Theologians Only!

Sermon on Hosea 4:4–10*

Yet let no one be upbraided and let no one be chastised, for it is you alone, O priest, whom I have to upbraid. Therefore you shall stumble by day and the prophet of the night shall stumble beside you. Therefore I will destroy your mother. My people are destroyed because they will not learn this. For you reject God's word and therefore I will reject you from being a priest to me. And since you have forgotten the law of your God, I also will forget your children. The more they increase, the more they sin against me; therefore I will turn their honor into shame. They feed on the sin of my people; they are greedy for their iniquity. And it shall be like people, like priest; for I will punish them for their ways, and requite them as they deserve: they shall eat and not be satisfied; they shall play the harlot and not multiply; because they have forsaken the Lord to cherish harlotry.

The people who are addressed here are priests—priests who have a heavy responsibility to God for their people. Priests in Israel are not on just the same footing as Jesus' disciples, or as twentieth-century theologians. They lived differently, and they also had a different mission and function. They did not have the same Word of God to proclaim as the messengers of Jesus. But it was the Word of the same God. Different people were entrusted to them. But their responsibility to God for these people was the same. So we twentieth-century theologians, together with all Jesus' disciples, move into the same front as Israel's priests. Like those priests we are subject to the same cutting word which Hosea addresses to them in God's name.

"Let no one be upbraided and let no one be chastised, for it is you alone, O priest, whom I have to upbraid"(v. 4). God talks in a special

---

*Preached at a weekday service in the theological seminary at Wuppertal on January 30, 1957.

way to theologians. This does not mean that, out of academic arrogance, they should have a particularly conceited view of themselves. The reason for God's address to them is that they have a primary responsibility. It is the lash of God's word that sets us apart. Do we perhaps imagine that we are specially close to God, in some bombproof shelter; or that we can shoot down all the others out of the impregnable fortress of a pulpit? We are under fire like no one else.

We are not merely under fire from all kinds of snipers. It may well be true that we are surrounded by critics, even if today we play safe and lay our black gowns aside. I am not saying that we should do better to put them on again. But what I do ask is: why don't we wear them? Do we simply want to pretend in public that we are the man in the street? Do we want to live more noncommittally? Are we evading our special responsibility out of cowardice? Or do we simply want to admit honestly that we are just people like everyone else, instead of dressing up the task we have been given? It is right that people should expect something special of us, because our whole lives are made over to our task. Our critics are altogether more justified in their criticism of us than we are in our criticism of them.

But our mandate comes from One who is more dangerous than this bombardment. He doesn't tackle the others first of all—the politicians and the capitalists, or any of society's favorite whipping boys. He takes the priests. Just as Jesus first of all takes his disciples, whom he sends out, and who disappoint him.

"Inner mobilization"—that is what this first of critics brings about. It is this that we theologians need on the eve of A.D. 2000—we teachers and clergy, and we students of theology. We have no right to an outward mobilization. Another will do that with us—or in spite of us. "Let no one be upbraided and let no one be chastised." What will not receive any fresh impetus is our criticism of congregational life and the life of the churches, or our judgment on the state and the economy, or all sectors of civilization and culture. That life is initially exonerated from our indictment. We do well first of all to stand in front of the world quite chastened and quite humbly. God's reprimand is addressed to *us*. The watchword is inner mobilization. God does not merely talk to us in words which we have to pass on to other people. Some of these words have us as their final destination.

Why are all the others exonerated? Because in the first place they are in a bad way just because God's messengers have not helped them as they should have done. The people who are guilty in this world are the ones who have despised and hidden the treasure with which they have been entrusted. What treasure? "You have rejected God's word; therefore will I reject you. You have forgotten the law of your God; therefore will I forget your kindred" (v. 6b). The prophet makes it crystal clear that the people who have received God's charge have to do one thing and one thing only: to live the Word of God which has been entrusted to them: to discern and proclaim God's acts on Israel's behalf and God's will for Israel. In exactly the same way Jesus' messengers are not asked what they have produced or what they have organized. The people of our generation are not asked, either, what ideas they have of their own or how extensive their activities are. We are simply and solely asked how we have acted towards the message of Jesus that has been entrusted to us. We owe the world no more than this. But this we very certainly do owe it. It is the living Word of God which has come among us in Jesus Christ, and which no one in our world can utter for himself. In the service of the living God there is nothing else to do but to bring the whole of life under his efficacious Word.

Jochen Klepper wrote in his diary on May 13, 1933: "Today the clergyman to whom Hanni applied for baptism called for the first time, after many weeks. All he had to offer was religious platitudes. Hanni knows a hundred times more about Christianity than pastors like this. Read the Bible!" One wonders what this pastor had had to do in all these weeks? If he had been living the message about the crucified Savior, he would surely not have come bringing religious platitudes. But what do we do? What will your generation do? "Read the Bible," Jochen Klepper writes for us in the family album; just what Hosea might have said. Deal with the Word of God, or better—discern how the Word of God deals with us. On New Year's Eve 1933, Klepper comes back from the church and writes: "Again I got nothing at all from the sermon. Don't the pastors sense how their sermons collapse as vain and empty things in the face of the words of the Bible that have been read to the congregation?" I would beg of you never to forget this: "Vain and empty things in the face of the words of the Bible that have been read." This self-complacency in the face of a crucified love! This playing with words in the face of a Word that calls the dead to life! This beating about the bush in the face of a clear assignment! The preaching of the Gospel in our time is in a poor way, and the person-to-person passing on of the Word is in a worse way still. And why? Because we find so little time for quiet listening. The life of us all stands and falls with the redeeming Word of our Lord. Indeed the life of us all is at stake in our everyday dealings with the Bible. Without this Word we theologians have neither meaning nor value on earth. The concern of our exegesis—the concern of our study of the history of the Word through the centuries—the concern of our questions about the task the Word is setting us today—is: the Word of Jesus. If we push the Word into the background, God will push us into the background too. If we lose interest in the Word, God will lose interest in us. God needs priests, disciples, and theologians because—and only because—the world needs his reconciling Word.

There can be no evasion here. All other activities can only increase the guilt we shall incur by abandoning the Word. Here the prophet puts his finger on three things:

1. The growing number of theologians. "The more they increase, the more they sin against me" (v. 7a). We must make sure that we do not come under the fire of this Word, with all our modern recruitment of young theological talent. In Israel, increasing prosperity under the early capitalism of the eighth century B.C. had multiplied the altars, just as among us new churches are growing up and with them new jobs for church personnel. But the church doesn't live from the great number of its witnesses. It lives from witnesses who are obedient. Better nine vacant churches and a single pastor who joyfully devotes himself heart and soul to the service of the Gospel rather than nine parishes occupied by nine vain and empty managers. Do we see how dangerous the magic of numbers is at a time when it does not seem to be exactly bad business to be a theologian? Do we sense among ourselves the danger of being so seduced by numbers that they encourage us and stimulate us to all kinds of things, but not to love of God's Word and to life with it? But things do not have to be like this. Numerous as we are, we do not have to make listening to the Word of the Lord more difficult for one another; we can also make it easier—something we love to do.

2. The way theologians make their living. "They feed on the sin of my people; they are greedy for their iniquity" (v. 8). Hosea has in mind the

fact that the priests encourage the business of sacrifice. They are pleased at every sin that is committed, recommending the people to make sacrifices in expiation. Levies of this kind also gave them a better livelihood. God's Word as Hosea knows it does not enjoin them to pursue this business. But they are doing so nonetheless because it increases their salary. Every one of us is in danger of shaping what he does in such a way that his life may be more advantageous, more lucrative, more enjoyable, irrespective of the real task itself. The old Adam finds it hard to see that it is not the fees or benefits and conveniences that are blessings in life, but solely devotion to the treasure of the Word of God. Jesus forbade his disciples to have silver or gold in their purses when they were engaged in his service. His saying "You cannot serve God and mammon" (Matt. 6:24) fits admirably into the instructions he gives his disciples. Among us the Word is in danger every day of being forgotten in favor of a more comfortable life. But the person for whom the Word is too narrow or too petty has still to learn that anything more is really less.

3. A very special sin committed by the priests of his time. "They play the harlot" (v. 10). "They exchange their honor for shame" (v. 7b). This is an attack on the Canaanite fertility cults which had been taken over by the priests and which in the prophet's view were pure "harlotry." They were exchanging the honor of God's Word for the shame of sultry rites. Their lasciviousness made these rites popular. Their antiquity and their wide dissemination showed that they were useful. By adopting them, God's people had subjected themselves to oriental guidelines for progress and utility. This temptation crops up in new form in every generation—the temptation for theologians to take as their standard what the public considers proven and what modern society finds plausible and congenial. But in all these competitive methods, with their psychological and organizational gimmicks, people remain shut up in their own worlds. The messenger of Jesus is squandering the talent with which he has been entrusted if he surrenders himself to these things. Clever programs of modern fertility cults, with their bustling activity, are a great temptation to us to despise God's simple words. Anyone who thinks that the address of the One whom all powers must obey is not effective enough will have to discover that all cheaply won effects are really futile.

One thing is certain, now and in the future: the church and its theologians do not live from numbers, or from more money, or from up-to-date ways of achieving success. They live only from the Word, which grows like a grain of mustard seed, which is the bread of life and the utterance of the final Victor. Our life and our work will be tested solely against the Word of Jesus Christ with which we have been entrusted. It is by that that we shall stand or fall.

Israel's priests are threatened that they will stumble even in daylight, because they have departed from the Word. The prophets who support them fare no better. The different title is no protection. They drag their families, even their mothers, down with them. "They shall eat and not be satisfied; they shall play the harlot and not multiply; because they have forsaken the Lord and do not regard him" (v. 10). The collapse of the office is the collapse of the person. In the John trial, the accused was the former president of the Office for the Protection of the Constitution. In giving judgment, the presiding judge said something which should give us theologians something to think about too: "The accused," he said, "held a particular office, and a very high one. The effect of the act he committed cannot be explained unless it is seen in conjunction with this high office. It is impossible to excuse someone who enjoys a high position by saying that he did not bring to his position the personal stature which the office really required. In this case there are only two alternatives. Anyone who occupies such a position without having the necessary caliber should resign from that position as soon as he becomes aware of his deficiency. If he does not resign his office, then the common weal requires that he shall be judged—personally as well—according to the standards which are appropriate for the holder of such a position."

Hosea has told us that the theologian's function is defined solely by the Word entrusted to him. We are all faced with the disquieting question: how does our personal stature measure up to the high office we hold? The New Testament message that judgment begins at the house of God can quickly have personal consequences for us. Of the people round Jesus, the one who is judged is not Pontius Pilate, not Herod, and not the High Priest; it is one of the Twelve—Judas. But the other one of the Twelve who turned to different methods—the sword and subterfuge—instead of to the Lord's Word allowed himself to be won back by his Lord's gaze: "Simon, son of John, do you love me?" (John 21:16).

The way that Peter took is the theologian's only hope. It is the way to the only Priest who lived nothing but the Word of God on earth and whose sacrifice was himself. In that sacrifice he vicariously suffered the death sentence passed on us faithless priests as well.

But his love does not give us carte blanche to go on fooling around. On the contrary, it calls us to himself, away from all evasions and all mistaken paths. He is the redeeming Word. He prepares his table for us in the presence of all our enemies. He holds out to us his supporting hand. The person who clings to it with his right hand, in the whirlpool of time, will have his left hand free to help other people. Amen.

10

This Ship Is Sinking!

Sermon on Amos 5:1–5*

Hear this word, you of the house of Israel!
    For I must begin to sing this dirge over you:
"Fallen, no more to rise,
    is the virgin Israel;
lies stretched forth on her own land,
    with none to raise her up."
For thus says the Lord God:
"The city that went forth as a thousand
    shall have a hundred back,
and that which went forth as a hundred
    shall have ten back."
For thus says the Lord to the house of Israel:
    "Seek me, then you shall live!
Do not seek Bethel!
    Go not to Gilgal!
For Gilgal shall go to the gallows,
    the house of God shall go to the devil."

Israel had no Sunday commemorating the dead or Eternity Sunday.[1] But it did have joyful feast days, especially in Amos's time. Defeats had been turned into victory. Economic slumps had been surmounted. People had time and money for cosmetics, for alcohol, for "gracious living." The religious festivals were welcome opportunities for crowning this life of glitter and luxury.

---

*Preached in the university service in the Peterskirche, Heidelberg, on the last Sunday in the church year, November 26, 1967.
[1] This last Sunday before Advent is known in the German churches as the Sunday of the Dead or Eternity Sunday.

And then this sheepbreeder turns up, this layman! He was certainly not wearing an academic gown or clerical vestments, and it was anything but according to plan when he transformed the festive bustle into a "Sunday of the Dead." "Virgin Israel"—yes, that is the right description! Isn't this nation still in the heyday of its youthful strength and beauty? But no: "Fallen, no more to rise, is the virgin Israel." Her own sated ground is her bier.

What incites Amos to this provocative dirge over so radiant a figure? Does he already see the Assyrians who in the next twenty or thirty years are going to flood over the country? No: one word only has thrust itself insistently into his ear, and it is this that he has to cry out. This is what the Lord has said:

> The city that went forth as a thousand
> shall have a hundred back,
> and that which went forth as a hundred
> shall have ten back.

Israel's militia is going to be decimated, hopelessly defeated. God's people is going to lose its state, its country, its men, women, and children, ". . . stretched forth on its land, and none to raise it up." And this is in fact just what happened, even if only after a few decades.

This was a different "Sunday of the Dead" from the one we have become accustomed to here. This was not a dirge for someone's nearest and dearest. This was not a "remember that you will die" addressed to the individual soul—or only insofar as these individuals belong to the Israel Amos was talking about. Jesus could still weep for the whole of Jerusalem. Luther got excited because the once flourishing Christian churches in Asia Minor and Africa had died out, and he warned Christians in Germany against complacency in the face of the driving rain of God's Word. And now the established church in Germany is encompassed by death—much more closely encompassed than in 1919—incomparably more dangerously than in 1934 and 1939. It is this for which Amos wants to open our eyes on this Sunday of the Dead. However virginal—or however old-maidish—our national churches may have been spruced up to look in their present constitution; however financially sound and however publicly influential they may be; and even if they linger on for another ten or twenty or thirty years, it must still be said now that our established church is down and out, ". . . fallen, no more to rise, is the virgin Israel." For it has long since become such a scattered throng that the only ministration that most people really wish it could receive is burial. Not even Amos's 10 percent have come back from the lost battle with the Enlightenment. When our university was inaugurated in 1386, with a mass in what was then the Chapel of the Holy Spirit, or when Ottheinrich reformed it with Melanchthon's help, you may be sure that hardly a single one of the professors and students would have been absent. How many of our twelve thousand students, seven hundred lecturers, and two hundred professors are here today? The "Humanistische Union," the "Spiegel," and many other groups are going to be less and less restrained with the slogans they shout. They are seeing to it, step by step, that however loudly the church bells may ring they won't be able to disguise how small and weak the Christian community really is. Even if here today the pews are full, we should not deceive ourselves about the general state of affairs in the churches up and down the country. Questions about the practice of levying a church tax and about the practice of infant baptism are not going to be put off any longer. The national church's own sated ground is going to be its bier.

Here clear-eyed faith must agree with unbelief in its assessment. Indeed it must outstrip unbelief in its judgment, and must exceed it in the clarity and distinctness of its perception:

> Fallen, no more to rise,
> is the virgin Israel.

It is high time to consider *this* death, which includes in itself all our living and our dying. A Christian society in its traditional form is disintegrating before our very eyes. Every wide-awake Christian, every budding theologian, and every church functionary must recognize the hour that has struck. The truth will make us free. *This ship is sinking.* We should stop being like the painters who, in Bertolt Brecht's words, are covering the walls of sinking ships with still lifes. How many thousand sermons up and down the country are doing just that? We have to show where the lifeboats and the life jackets are. More: we have to learn, like Peter, how to walk on the water without drowning. The question remains: what about our faith, when the last churchbells have stopped ringing after the next thirty years? This is the only question for which we need an answer.

And the answer is given us by Amos in the words that follow his terrible assessment:

Seek me, then you shall live!

"Then you shall live." That is what we should hear first of all. It is on this that the emphasis falls, after the dirge for the dead is finished. Individual people clutched at what Amos said and kept it alive and safe, even after Israel's death. When the proud annals of imperial Assyria sank into dust and ashes, this saying, like other prophetic sayings, remained alive and woke people to new life. The kingdom of Judah was destroyed too. This word gathered round itself those who had been scattered and taught them to hope. The life appeared which no death could fetter. Empires came and went. The crucified Jesus went as rescuer through them all into the future, with the word of his messengers. He proved himself to be the only liberator, when even the votaries of enlightened reason went down like ninepins before the superior force of wickedness—proved himself most strongly perhaps when in the Third Reich the mainstream churches already lay waste and broke up inwardly, when congregations gathered together in factories, on hard garden chairs, when over the parade ground of a concentration camp the voice of a dying man cried out of the cellar: "I know that my Redeemer lives."

The promise of life has proved its force and *it remains in force*. To us today the total collapse of our church tradition must be ruthlessly clear; but at that very point we also receive the promise of life. Yes, only here can we hear it in its full force as the call of the only free Lord. The Lord of Israel does not die with Israel, as the gods die with their own nations and their own phases of history. The Lord of the Christian faith is the creator and master of all life, of all change, of all future; God does not live from our traditions. We are now faced with the question of whether we are going to cling to those dying traditions. I see some of us older people weary of life, even sickened at it—"fed to the teeth," as we say. It is more than these people can stand when they see incomprehensible attacks flaring up. Which of the young ones is still going to feel like

94

changing over from the imposing ocean liner into our insecure little boat? But above those of us who are resigned and above those of us who are afraid stands the promise: "Then you shall live." But we first of all have to lay hold of this totally independent offer of life for ourselves.

We should lay hold of it for the sake of everyone. The life it means is a life that is serenely cheerful, contented, and complete. We do not as yet find it in the places where today "the necessity of peace" is rightly thought about and preached, because this is the only reasonable course. The will and the hope for peace certainly do not exist merely because we men and women today can no longer live without them. Who is going to prevent people from again despairing over people? Who is going to stop the awakening perception that peace is compulsively necessary from swinging over to pessimism, cynicism, and murderous or suicidal psychosis? A contented life and the will and hope for peace can only endure where the unreliability of human beings enters realistically into the calculation. But above the unreliability of human beings stands the shining offer of the Lord of all: you shall live, even you, unstable as water though you are! This offer withstands death. In its very dying, Israel, and with Israel the church, the world of the nations, and every member of humanity, is allowed to accept it as the gift of completion and perfection.

How do we receive it on behalf of the world around us and for ourselves? How do we receive it, in the death of our established church and in the decline of Christian tradition—this serenity of living, this completeness, this blitheness shared, not by first-class passengers on the sinking liner, but by the survivors in the little boat, by people who are walking on the water? Amos tells us precisely: "Seek me, then you shall live!" Who is the One who is crying: seek *me*?

Amos gives us three answers here. First of all, he is the Lord of judgment. Seek after the One who has decreed that these things shall die. Amos uses very plain words:

> Do not seek Bethel!
>   Go not to Gilgal!
> For Gilgal shall go to the gallows,
>   the house of God shall go to the devil.

Many people in Germany have a story to tell about their experience with the established church. I wouldn't know how to prevent it if one of these people were to translate Amos into different words:

> Leave the church
>   and drop its services!
> Its pious forms and canting tales
>   are merely fossils and dead as doornails.

Let me warn you in all seriousness against any kind of Pharisaism toward voices like this. They could well be closer to the prophet than many a worthy churchgoing Christian.

It is true: Bethel and Gilgal once meant a great deal in the history of God's people. Let me put it in the strongest possible terms. Our established churches meant great things in the past—indeed the greatest things of all—for me, and for many others among us, as they did for our forefathers. We found in them the best thing in life. In Bethel the heavens opened for Jacob and he received the mighty promise of his God. Gilgal was the bridgehead to the promised land, a memorial to the liberation from slavery and from the sea and the waters of Jordan, which meant from the powers of chaos. And yet the golden calf now stands in Bethel, and what is celebrated in Gilgal is personal achievement. That is why Amos says that God wants to be distinguished from the venerable places of his great acts. The God of faith moves on and changes things. He once left Shiloh, and he will one day leave Jerusalem, said Jeremiah later. He will be wholly identified with the one who was executed outside the gates of Jerusalem, far from the sanctuary. He can turn away from academic chairs and orthodox pulpits. We ourselves are taking too short-term a view if we put down the attacks on our present-day ecclesiastical institutions to human shortsightedness and stupidity.

So the first answer is: seek the one who pronounces his unerring judgment on your traditions. Learn to distinguish between your traditions and his living will. Seek me myself, the judge, then you shall live, says the Lord.

But how are we to distinguish between him and the spirit of the age? Elsewhere Amos suggests that the answer is seek me as the Lord of the beginnings. Take your bearings entirely from what he began, not from what men and women have made of it.

"Did you bring to me sacrifices and offerings the forty years in the wilderness?" we read later in our chapter. I have exerted myself for you in your weakness, "I drove out the Amorites before you, whose height was like the height of the cedars, and who were as strong as the oaks." I was always on the side of the weak and the little, unimportant people. "I have chosen you out of all the families of the earth." This is how Amos reminds his people of their beginnings.

If there is one thing we have to take with us out of the big ship into the little boats, then it is the Word about the beginnings, the Word of the prophets and apostles, the message of Jesus Christ, who puts himself on the side, not merely of the weak and oppressed, but even on the side of the guilty—who indeed actually takes their place. For here the still unattained goal of the future comes into view. So for us, "seek me" means: examine the Scriptures with fresh energy and in complete quiet. You need them as helmsmen for finding the proper direction, as oarsmen, to give strength. We must return in a completely new way to a daily, attentive reading of Holy Scripture. That early Christian watchword about standing fast in the teaching of the apostles proved itself in the maneuvers of the thirties and forties: do not let a day pass without God's word!

For this we need perseveringly enquiring Bible study groups. They are as necessary as daily bread, everywhere in the boat crews, in student groups, in house cells. For this some of the work of the established church can still be of help, as long as there is still time. This is *the* preparation for taking to the boats. Anyone who knows himself knows how necessary this intensive, prayerful gathering round the biblical Word is for everyone. Anyone who knows our surrounding world today knows that, more than anything else, we owe it the new spirit that comes to us from this regular meditation.

Just as the helmsman looks at the compass and the chart, so we can find our bearings by studying the Word of the prophets and apostles. Just as the rowers are bound to look backward, so we have to look toward the Lord of the beginnings, who has been testified to us, if we are really to move forward and to arrive at the proper destination. For the Lord of the beginnings is the present judge and the Lord of the future. So "seek me" means, second, seek in the Scriptures—but seek *me* in the Scriptures. Then you shall live!

We must take still one more, final step. I must say quite explicitly that it is a hazardous step, but it is unavoidable. Amos himself knows without any doubt that he has been mastered, vanquished by his God. Anyone who rejects *his* cutting judgment is rejecting *his God*. The prophet does not cry out his message in intoxicated ecstasy or because it brings him any personal advantage or out of professional routine. He *has* to cry out: "Thus says the Lord!" He has to do so because, for the day in which he is living, the God of the beginnings is the judge who is present—present in the prophetic Word which Amos now proclaims.

So today "seek me" means, third: ask about the people who have been mastered. People who have been vanquished by the Word of the Lord have been given to us today too, in a marvelous way. They point us to the boats which can safely reach the shore that has no landing-stage for the ocean liner. There are some living witnesses like this in the worldwide church, and there are some among us too. Like Amos once, and like Jesus, they are all too easily viewed as outsiders. But they are God's gifts to the world. I need only name here Eugene Carson Blake, the [then] General Secretary of the World Council of Churches. He calls his government's terrible use of force in Vietnam the greatest danger for the whole of humanity and its future, a wicked desecration of the name of Christian in the world. Our established churches as a whole have remained silent about this, just as they in general remained silent about the murder of the Jews, although today the fate of all the nations is inextricably linked. Amos in his time did not remain silent when the Moabites dealt infamously with the dead body of an Edomite king. Although he was a Judaean, it was not a matter of indifference to him when Aramaeans waged a cruel war in Gilead. Are we permitted to hold our tongues when, last week alone, fourteen hundred Vietnamese were torn in pieces by American bombs during those frightful battles for Hill 875—fourteen hundred young people, far more than are gathered together here in this church today, and in addition numberless women and children, who are reduced to misery and fated to die? Let no one say that it has nothing to do with us Christians in Germany when other Christians carry this cruel, mass slaughter into other countries. We are asked whether we will not at long last in the twentieth century comprehend and testify to the way of the crucified Jesus, who commanded that the sword be sheathed, as the way of salvation for the whole of mankind. Our churches do not in general draw *the* long overdue conclusion for us: to call all their members in the name of the crucified Jesus to resolute service for peace, and to a rejection of the use of force everywhere. It is not merely for the people who "sit under" us preachers that the established church is, largely speaking, a desert. It is a desert in the pulpits too. We are all, for the most part, living as if we were muzzled dogs, instead of being watchmen on the walls, where the very stones have long since cried out. So "seek me" means too: *seek*, where water springs forth from the rock in the desert, where it is not yesterday's rotten, stinking manna which has been stored up and handed round, but where the fresh manna falls for today. We must *seek* for the proper ways of worship. Too many people have already given up the search in resignation and do not come to church at all. All those responsible must get together and think about this. And they should consider the services here, in the Peterskirche, which offer such a splendid opportunity. We must struggle to hear the living Word of the living Lord, and to pass it on. At the moment the boats and the life jackets which everyone needs are still on the ship. We must seize the opportunity. Seek the messengers who have been mastered by the service of reconciliation, but seek *me* among them, says the Lord. Seek in the Scriptures for the Lord of the beginnings, as the One who is to come; seek *me myself* in the Scriptures, says the Lord. Distinguish between your pious traditions and my present will—seek *me myself*, says the Lord.

I could finish this sermon by stripping off my clerical collar in front of you, and by unbuttoning my gown, taking it off here in the pulpit, and tearing it into twelve pieces, as Ahijah of Shiloh once did, as a sign that only one tribe would remain to the house of Solomon—that is to say, that Jerusalem's supporters would be decimated. I could let the rags of my gown flutter down at your feet. In this way too we should probably move closer to Amos and to Jesus than to the priests who opposed them. So at the Church Assembly in episcopal Hanover, I insisted on preaching in the sport stadium without a gown. But true renewal never began with the ceremonies; the Reformation taught us that. What would be gained? The age of demonstrations would merely be enriched by one little spectacle more.

But what would be hampered would be the one thing necessary, which today gathers us round the table of Jesus, and which we will take with us when we part again until next Sunday: the personal resolve, under the eyes of our Lord, that for each of us the week will be determined by the one exclusive sentence: "Seek me, then you shall live," says the Lord. Every one of us has to tear up the traditions and customs he idolizes. Every one of us, just in his ordinary clothes, is permitted to enquire from the Word of the prophets and apostles about the will of the coming Lord. Everyone is supposed to seek, and to invite others to the preaching of the messengers who have been overpowered by God. For everything which the world needs has been in our midst ever since Jesus: life that is serenely cheerful, contented, and complete.

The peace of God, which guards all our thinking, will keep your thoughts and resolves in Christ Jesus.

Let us pray:
Lord our God,
you offer us free, new life.
We thank you for the overmastering power of your forgiveness.
Our thinking and our hands are lazy.
Help us to seek your gifts with fresh zeal,
    daily in the Word of your messengers,
    every Sunday in the congregation of your people,
    and that as we do these things your Spirit may enter into
        lordship over us.
We pray for all the congregations of your people, especially
        for student congregations, that they may not curtail the breadth
        of your unconditional love and may not withhold it from
        anyone.
We beseech you for the unspeakable misery of the Vietnamese
        people. Give peace, sooner than we dare to hope.
Strengthen the will of all Christians, resolutely to renounce
        the use of force.
We pray for our university and for all colleges and universities
        in Germany,
    that helpful reforms may be fostered,
    that trust may grow between students and teachers,
    that even angered professors and extremist student groups

may be able to find a way to one another through practical
and objective work,
that we may all be able to work in peace for the good of
all mankind,
that in the trials in Berlin[2] all the people concerned may
seek only for justice and righteousness, and that they may
respect their opponents.
But to us all give strength, so that we may be the witnesses
and helpers of a life that has been brought to harmony and
peace. Amen.

---

[2] Legal proceedings in connection with the student revolts which took place at this time.

11

Disputed Old Testament

An Epilogue (1956)

In my opinion it is not Christian to want to take our thoughts and feelings too quickly and too directly from the New Testament.

Dietrich Bonhoeffer,
Letters and Papers from Prison

These sermons are meant to render an account. People often remonstrate with us academic teachers of theology, asking skeptically: how do you move from your scholarly exegesis to proclamation? Don't you detain your theological students unnecessarily with philological and historical erudition? The answer can only be that it is impossible to expend too much industry on trying to discover with all the means available what the biblical words actually say and want to convey. For there is a great danger that we will read our own wishes into the Bible, as well as ideas that are really alien to it. And the only way we can be helped to avoid this is by listening to what God's witnesses really wanted to say.

Of course it is quite possible to stop short halfway in this laborious process. This is undoubtedly the danger that confronts us every day—the danger of all "scribes": the danger of straining at gnats and swallowing camels, of disputing about the letter and burying the treasure with which we have been entrusted. The work of explaining the text is often so laborious that the preaching of it can get lost in the process. And yet the hour always comes when the text itself drives us to preaching. And we are challenged too by the congregation, and by the need of men and women round about us. So then the silence must be broken, and research and enquiry must turn into a passing on to other people. It is no wonder that the outcome is nothing more than a provisional attempt. But it is still, as it always has been, the mighty act of our God to

103

create full and perfect help and to bring his people to their goal, through inadequate instruments.

Old Testament preaching is evidently having a particularly difficult time at the moment. Some of us see the danger of the Old Testament's slowly but surely becoming a second-class section of Holy Scripture, because it plays far too small a part in the actual proclamation of the gospel. Are people afraid that the joyful message of Jesus Christ will be cut short? There may be some basis for this view, for we live side by side with Jews who, with the Old Testament in their hand, pass Jesus by. And can we ourselves honestly understand the Old Testament historically unless we deliberately leave Jesus Christ out?

But the reverse is just as true. What happens in the New Testament? Evangelists and apostles cannot present Jesus of Nazareth to us as the Christ of God and the savior of all mankind without continually citing the Old Testament. When the first Christians preached Christ, from Peter's Pentecost sermon onward, they took as their texts chapters from the Old Testament. Anyone who searches for conviction about the things of Jesus will, like the people in Berea, search daily in the Old Testament "whether those things were so" (Acts 17:11). The history of Christianity shows that people go very badly astray when they try to know and follow Jesus Christ while at the same time shutting up the Old Testament. What remains is merely a Christ philosophy. The real Jesus to whom the New Testament calls us points us everywhere to the Old.

But then what is really valid—the Old Testament of the Jews without Jesus Christ, or Jesus Christ with the Old Testament? Anyone who has taken up the Old Testament in Jesus' name can only discover that, as the document of a thousand years of history, it crumbles away in our hands if we do not have Jesus before our eyes as its point of orientation. But for the person who looks toward Jesus Christ, the Old Testament begins to speak in a new way. Without Jesus, we see distorted proportions, blurred contours, and confused lines, as we do through clouded glass. With him we see the clear historical reality, testimonies to God's dealings with his people and to the life of men and women under God and without God; and in the most manifold ways all these testimonies serve one thing: to help us grasp the meaning and purpose of the mission of Jesus Christ in all its riches, and to lead us into practical life with him.

When we open the Old Testament for Jesus' sake, the real point is that we should achieve true life with him in the historical reality of this present world. We must remember and practice the suggestions Dietrich Bonhoeffer gave us in his last letters: "This world must not be prematurely written off; in this the Old and New Testaments are at one" (*Letters and Papers from Prison*, p. 337). "God's 'beyond' is not the beyond of our cognitive faculties. The trancendence of epistemological theory has nothing to do with the transcendence of God. God is beyond in the midst of our life. The church stands, not at the boundaries where human powers give out, but in the middle of the village. That is how it is in the Old Testament, and in this sense we still read the New Testament far too little in the light of the Old" (p.282). "In my opinion it is not Christian to want to take our thoughts and feelings too quickly and too directly from the New Testament. . . . One cannot and must not speak the last word before the last but one. We live in the last but one and believe the last, don't we?" (p.157). Yes, because in what is next to last we have to live in the discipleship of Jesus Christ in the direction of the Christ who is to come, we need the Old Testament too as our canon.

This still leaves many individual questions open. Some of them need to be clarified at a fundamental level; I am including here one attempt to do this which grew out of discussions with students. Other problems can only be solved in each given case, by means of careful attention to the texts. It is as attempts of this kind that these sermons are intended. They are not based on any generally valid recipe. But at the same time I have kept to three simple rules, which I have never found it possible to evade: first, to enquire as carefully as possible into the historical meaning of the text, so that the situation of the witness and his listeners and, above all, the intention of his message may be exactly and distinctly grasped; second, to compare the Old Testament text with corresponding New Testament passages and the center of their kerygma, so as to show how far the Old Testament message elucidates the message of the New, and how far the one has been superseded by the other; third, to seek out, with the message of the text, those people to whom that text speaks, among the listeners to the sermon, so that the original kerygmatic intention of the text—and thus the will of the living God today—is not buried, either under history or under philosophy.

It is in this sense that I also understand the "typological" interpretation which has meanwhile come to seem indispensable, even though this programmatic expression is disputed and frequently misunderstood, tradition having encumbered it with so much ballast. For me, typological interpretation therefore means:

1. historical interpretation (as distinct from allegory);

2. comparative interpretation which draws on New Testament analogies (as distinct from targumistic paraphrase and rabbinical casuistry);

3. kerygmatic interpretation (as distinct from an exclusively historical exegesis).

Finally, I must acknowledge that the wealth of problems presented by the Old Testament has anything but diminished my pleasure in the riches of this unique book. On the contrary, the joy has only thereby been increased. So I may also dare to hope that the texts expounded here may play their part in arousing new delight and new love for the *whole* Bible.

12

Some Thoughts on the Typological Interpretation of the Old Testament

THESES (1956)

I. The Premises

1. In all strata of the New Testament writings, the New Testament kerygma can only recognize and acknowledge Jesus of Nazareth as the Christ of God by way of more or less explicit reference to the Old Testament. Knowledge of Jesus Christ and knowledge of the Old Testament go hand in hand in early Christian testimony.

2. The fundamental features of the Old Testament's testimony to God find no correspondence, historically, either in the religions of Israel's neighbors or in later Jewish history. It is the New Testament alone which offers an analogy —the analogy of a testimony of faith based on historical facts, telling of the will toward covenant of the God who chooses a people out of the midst of the world and calls it to liberty under his rule.

3. If we compare the Old Testament testimony about God's purpose with Israel, and its testimony about the path taken by Israel, we can see that it is incomplete. It waits for the future, for fulfillment, for God's final act in Israel.

II. The Necessity of Typological Interpretation

1. We do not have a direct and unbroken relationship to the words of the Old Testament writings because we ourselves are neither Israel nor are we living before Christ.

2. But we cannot belong to Jesus Christ and live in the church of the New Testament without reading the Old Testament together with Jesus and together with that early Christian community.

3. The pre-Christian kerygma in Israel applies to us because it testifies to the same God who manifests himself in Christ as the God of Israel and of all the nations.

4. The New Testament listens to Old Testament prophecy for what it has to say about Christ, but it sees that Testament also as the path along which God guides Israel *toward* Christ and, finally, finds in it the exemplary manifestation of God's will in his history with Israel. So the New Testament hears what the Old has to say about Christ, but also what it tells about the life of God's people and the life of men and women before God. All in all, therefore, the Old Testament is for the New the book of God's revelation, the book of life under God. According to the New Testament's understanding, we grasp too little about the Old if we interpret it merely as a book of promise pointing to Christ.

5. According to our understanding today, the Old Testament certainly points forward, largely speaking; but for all that, it is not merely prophecy. It witnesses to the acts God performed in the past for Israel and the world of the nations, and to the acts he will perform in the future for Israel and for mankind, in judgment and salvation; and it is a witness to the life of God's people. All in all, therefore, the Old Testament is not a book of prophecy; it is a testimony to the acts of God, past and to come, and to the life of the people of God under the God who has been manifested.

6. This means that the total kerygma of the Old Testament is not properly understood, either according to the witness of the New Testament or according to our present understanding,
   a) if it is interpreted wholly and exclusively as promise,
   b) if it is seen essentially as being a contrast, a clarifying antithesis, to the New Testament,
   c) if it is considered to be identical with the New Testament message in its essential content and is therefore interpreted allegorically.

7. Both the New and the Old Testaments demand, rather, an interpretation of the Old Testament which
   a) understands that Testament, in accordance with the historical facts, as being the testimony of God's revelation in Israel before Christ's birth;

b) perceives the historical and kerygmatic connection between the Testaments, through which the Old Testament indirectly acquires meaning for the New Testament people of God;

c) discerns the historical and kerygmatic difference between the Testaments, and therefore finds in the Old Testament a provisional, preparatory and exemplary testimony.

The New Testament recognizes that the happenings of the Old Testament continue to have significance in the period of the New Covenant; and it defines this significance through the word *typikōs* (1 Cor. 10:11). We therefore call the interpretation which corresponds to these facts "typological." Typological interpretation finds analogies to the New Testament in the Old;

that is to say, it finds

what is comparable, in spite of differences;

what is valid, especially in what is provisional;

what is contradictory or in contrast, in the continual

progression of God's living activity.

III. Principles of Typological Interpretation

1. The historical meaning of an Old Testament text must be investigated with all the methods available to philological and historical scholarship.

2. The *scopus*, or theme, or kerygma, of the Old Testament witness must be determined. We must also expect that, in many Old Testament passages, the *scopus* will only emerge in a wider literary context, beyond the limits of the passage in question.

3. The *pericope*, or passage under consideration, with its *scopus* (its theme, kerygma) must be seen in its total biblical context as a piece of history preceding the Christ event to which the New Testament testifies. Accordingly, the determinative question for a real understanding is: what does the Old Testament text in its historical meaning have to say to the men and women who are living under the New Covenant with Jesus Christ? The protean character of the Old Testament texts means that there are many different kinds of answers to this question:

a) The Old Testament text reveals provisionally the will, the motive, and the intention of the God of Israel, who has lastly and finally accepted his people and all peoples in Jesus Christ. Thus the Old Testament text helps us to see God at work in Jesus Christ. The Old Testament texts show the Christ event as the divine eschatological event. The Old Testament helps to preserve the church's witness to Christ from a false historicization.

b) The Old Testament text shows in specific historical situations a foreshadowing of the manifestation of God which became final and ultimate history in Jesus Christ. Thus the Old Testament text helps us to see more clearly the specific meaning and the true significance of the mission of Jesus Christ among us. With the help of the Old Testament text the historical function of the Christ event is elucidated. In the light of the Old Testament the church's witness to Christ is kept from degenerating into a Christ philosophy and an analysis of existence.

c) The Old Testament text puts before us exemplary cases drawn from God's people. In this way it helps us to discern rightly the nature and commission of the church as the body of Christ in the midst of history. In the light of the Old Testament text the Christ event is perceived as being God's act for God's people. With the help of the Old Testament the church's witness to Christ is preserved from false individualization.

d) The Old Testament text offers examples of ways taken by God's people, instances of their acts, situations, decisions, sufferings, aberrations, and deliverances. In this way it helps the church to find the path of practical faith and obedience. In the light of the Old Testament text the Christ event is recognized as the gift of God which we have to believe and lay hold of, as God's last Word and ultimate help, in the provisional and this-worldly condition of history. The Old Testament helps to preserve the church's witness to Christ from a false transcendentalization.